TALES OF TOILS

Collaborative Works

By: McConnell Middle School

6th Grade Students in Ms. Alicia Piascik's

Class - 2017

(Fourth Period)

3G Publishing, Inc.

Loganville, Ga 30052

www.3gpublishinginc.com

Phone: 1-888-442-9637

First published by 3G Publishing, Inc. May, 2017

ISBN: 9781941247402

Printed in the United States of America

Contents

Contributors

Jared Archer

Nicholas Arcila

Lily Asbee

Zarmeena Azmat

Jacob Ball

Gabriel Brown

Anna Burnett

Emma Busboom

Keighley Byrd

Tyler Callaway

Jacob Chandler

Seth Chase

Cadie Cooper

Erin Eakin

Jackson Foster

Sydney Harris

Mary Horton

Katherine Lyons

Evan McCarty

Amanda Robinson

Gabrielle Schlicker

Andrew Schnufp

Abigail Schwindt

Nathan Smith

CHAPTER 1

The Struggles are Real

By: Jared Archer

Hi, I'm Salbert Meinstein, you know me 30 year old millionaire scientist who found the cure for pretty much every modern-day disease. A I am going to tell you about my life and all the struggles that lie within. Let's start with when I was a child. I was seven years old when I first became obsessed with the science, after watching this awesome video called Bill Nye the Science Guy. Later on, on my eighth birthday my parents got me a really cool science kit that came with the book.

The book has all the science experiments, and the kit has all the materials you need to do the experiments. The first experiment I did was making a floating Lantern. Paper, matches, small candle, and a candle holder with the materials that called for. When I first started I set my hopes too high. The first time I thought it was easy so I got done quickly. So I thought. I didn't set it up right and one side fell in, and then the whole paper caught on fire luckily I had a hose close to me and there were lots of backup papers. Next trial failed, 3rd failed, 4th failed, 5th failed. Then I started my 6th things started great it started to lift off, but got 1 inch off the ground, stayed for a couple of seconds then fell to the ground and caught on fire again. Now up to my 12th trial then failed. I was really struggling and almost gave up. But I worked through it! Then finally on the 20th trial, it worked it flew off and I found 1 block down the street. Like Thomas Edison said " I have not failed ten thousand times. I've just found   ten thousand ways that won't work." Now let's fast forward 20 years. Look at me at Georgia Tech on my last year until I got my doctorate degree in all science. Today was the day of the final exam. There were 100 questions plus an essay and we had three hours to finish all of that.

"You may beginning your tests now" exclaimed the teacher. 1-A, 2-B, 3-C, 10 minutes later, 33-B, 34-B, 35-D. 30 minutes after that, "Yes done with the questions, there's an essay that's right!!" "Ugh" It was a five paragraph essay. I looked at the time and said "whoa" surprised that I had 2 hours and 20 minutes left. after 2 paragraphs in I got a major hand cramp! It took me 45 minutes to get through those two paragraphs. But the hand cramp made me get through another 2 paragraphs in 1 hour and 5 minutes. My hand hurt really bad, I had to stop writing,for 10 minutes then I realized I only have 20 minutes left.

I struggled but 10 minutes went by and I had five sentences down and 2 to go another five minutes went by and I was done I shouted in my mind "YES I'M DONE!!!" It was hard but I pushed through and hopefully it pays off. I anx

iously waited for 3 weeks. When the mail arrived, I looked at the score and it was a big fat 100!!!

I celebrated with my family the following week. 7 years later I had a job interview to be the scientist I always wanted to be, a medical researcher! later that week they called and let me know that I was hired, and that I could start next Monday. I asked if I could bring my stuff in and then they said yes, if you would like to I said thank you for the job and hung up. The next Monday I clocked in at the front desk and went to my office. Bing! I had gotten an email, from who I wonder. I open the email and it said

Dear Dr. Meinstein,

I would like to say welcome to the S.O.A (Scientists of America) and also give you and your team (Dr. Huertas and Dr. Schnupp) an assignment. I want you three to find a cure for, you guessed it, Cancer. Thanks for helping. Good luck!!!

Signed, Dr. Yoder

Wow this guy means business! But how, how are we going to find a cure for cancer? "Hey Salbert" exclaimed Schnupp "Hey Salbert" exclaimed Huertas. "Hey team, welcome. Come in, come in! Have a seat!"Then I shook both of their hands. After they sat down in I asked them about the project. Schnupp let me know this would be a lot of work, and he asked me if I was sure I was in for the job still I told him yes so he clapped once and then said "Let's get to work!" So first we stop by Mr. Yoders and told him we were going to get to work. " Great" he exclaimed. After stopping by Mr. Yoders we headed over to the lab. I was the leader of the team so I basically told the team what not to do, and what to do.

"So team, this is going to be very difficult, but we will push through and finally get a cure for cancer!" "I like your tone of voice" mentioned Dr. Huertas! "I agree" Schnupp said as he got to work. "All right, let's start by adding with potassium hydrogen tartrate with dinitrogen oxide. That will come together and make what I like to call NABON O. Then we add some sodium phosphate to the NABON O, and that should come out to be what we need" I predicted. "But first we need to test it" I voiced! The next week the three of us went to a hospital. After we walked we got a little creeped out, because there were only the emergency lights on. But then we realized that they were on because all the patients were having time where they can rest without the lights being on.

"Hmm, this place isn't so weird after all" Dr. Huertas "Let's go and ask around to see if anyone with cancer would like to try out our medicine." Knock! Knock! "Who is it" exclaimed a patient in pain. "We are Dr. Meinstein, Dr. Huertas, and Dr. Schnupp" we all exclaimed! " And we are here to help you over through the Cancer disease!" " No, I was born with Cancer and I'm going to die with Cancer" shouted the patient! Right then and there I thought to myself am I just going to be a big bust? Is everyone like this? I hope not or that would be a struggle, because I spent my whole life studying science? But the next couple of years were amazing we finally found the right ingredients to cure the huge disease Cancer! As you can see now all of my study actually paid off. BIGTIME!!!

CHAPTER 2

The Chronicles Of Isaac

By: Nicholas Arcila and Seth Chase

Once upon a time… there was a 12 year old boy with brown hair, piercing blue eyes, and a lanky frame, named Isaac. He lived with his mom, dad, and 3 older cocky brothers on a farm. They lived in poverty and Isaac lived in sadness. His brothers were big, strong, and fast, unlike him, and therefore Isaac was hated by the village. One day, a guard came riding up on a horse to the farm yelling "I'm here for Isaac!" Isaac, petrified with fear, came up to the guard remembering stories of boys the king took who never came back. The guard introduced himself as Edward and said he would bring Isaac to the king who would explain everything.

However, on their way there, they were attacked! A big, hideous, three headed troll blocked them. With a savage roar from the monster their horse grunted and galloped off. Edward pulled out his bow and quickly shot the heathen in one of six eyes. This, however, just made the beast angry as it charged at them. Edward swiftly stabbed it, causing the beast to turn around swinging its fist. **"CRACK!"** went Edward's jawbone. The poor man fell to the ground screaming in pain. Then, some guards from a nearby village arrived with crude spears and swords. They ganged up on the beast, stabbing and slicing as it flailed around, until all was silent.

Unexpectedly, an old lady dressed in rags came out throwing healing potions on all of the fallen guards including Edward. One hour later, the effects of the potion healed Edward and both he and Isaac went on their way. The pair then came to a sketchy village. They paid two gold coins to buy and leave their horse at a stable and to buy rooms at a lodge. After they had fallen asleep, Isaac awoke to footsteps in his room, and saw a bandit standing there knife drawn. Isaac grabbed his safety weapon, a small pocket dagger and threw it with all his might, catching the man in the skull. The man collapsed, and Edward rushed in after hearing the noise. The guard then left when he saw the disturbance had been taken care of.

The next morning he informed Isaac, "the creatures and people we have fought are nothing compared to what is coming." Isaac shivered. Edward stepped outside and then Isaac heard a man talking to Edward, followed by the guard yelling, "What do you mean my horse was stolen!" Then, Edward stormed out, with Isaac following him to buy a new horse. After buying a new horse the guard said to keep quiet as they were going into a monster infested forest.

During their journey Isaac said, "This place is creepy." The guard shushed him, but it was too late. A massive 10 ft. tall, young Ent (living evil tree) had awoken! It charged at them, but with a spur of the guard's heel, their horse dodged tricking the Ent into slamming into a tree. The Ent chased them through the forest. The horse was faster, but the Ent knew the terrain better. Finally, they left the forest leaving the tree monster's comfort zone so it retreated.

On the way to the castle, Edward was silent while Isaac slept, until they arrived where he rudely awakened Isaac with a punch to the arm. Isaac said "ow", while the guard said "let's go." In the throne room, Isaac met with King Frank who told him, "You will be my gladiator." A royal guard led Isaac to a room with battle equipment after dinner *(where Isaac cried and said nothing nor ate anything because of fear.)* Then the guard told Isaac "Get ready, for your life depends on it."

As Isaac stepped into the hot arena, he realized about 1,000 nobles were watching him. With his sword and shield, he hoped his armor would protect him. Then, a chant started "5, 4, 3, 2, 1", and the gates lifted. A hideous creature emerged out. **"A MANTICORE!"** Isaac shouted.

The body was the shape and size of a regular lion, but with a distorted human face, as well as metal segmented tail with a poisonous spiky ball at the tip. Then it roared, a bone chilling sound, creating a wave of the smell of rotten meat. Then the creature shot a volley of poisonous spikes out of its tail. Isaac used his natural reflexes to block with his shield. It saved his life but turned the shield into wooden splinters. Then, he surprised the manticore by charging it and attempting to stab its hideous face. But the manticore used its tail, which had regrown its spikes, to knock the sword out of Isaac's hand.

Excitedly the manticore rose up to crush its opponent who rolled out of the way just in time. Looking around

Isaac grabbed a spike where the poison had slid to the end. In a blaze of fury at the manticore for almost taking his life, he threw the spike hitting the manticore in the face. Seconds later the poison kicked in causing the violent beast to crash to the floor dead. Isaac was then informed he had another battle coming and would be equipped again.

Readying for his second fight, Isaac geared up. **"Today son, you will be fighting, the UNDEFEATED POISON SPITTER!"** King Frank exclaimed. "I'm ready sir!" Isaac shouted **"10,9,8,7,6,5,4,3,2,1,0, FIGHT!!!"**, the king's men shouted. The gate opened, the chains are released and a nasty snake came out looking feisty and fearful. Laying long, at 38ft, its body had an orange coat of scales protecting it, three horns on its head, another head on the opposite side of the body, and the beast seemed extremely angry. The snake rapidly lunged at Isaac, who barely managed to roll out of the way. While Isaac was dodging, the other head surprised him from behind! Wrapping around him, the snake began to squeeze like a constrictor. Isaac plunged his sword deep into its flesh surrendering his sword. When it released, he ran. Then, he realized why the creature was undefeated and called the "Poison Spitter," As it spat poison out of its fangs at him. The poison splattered his helmet and chest plate, forcing Isaac to whip them off. Then, when the snake hissed, Isaac threw the ruined equipment into its mouths. Causing it to make a gurgling sound. Then its orange scales turned green, and it fell to the ground dead.

Isaac now figured that this was not the end of his quest. After a brief rest, Isaac was once again summoned to the Royal Arena at King Frank's castle. As he put on his armor, the king's servant gave him his shield and sword. The king's guards started a countdown to release the next monstrosity: a Chimera! The crowd then counted down, **"7, 6, 5, 4, 3, 2, 1, RELEASE!!!!"** The Chimera that Isaac was fighting was 5 feet tall at the top of the head, 10 feet long at the tip of its snake tail, had a lion body and face, and a goat head on its back. The battle then began and the crowd yelled: **"ATTACK!!!!"**

The Chimera grunted and groaned, ready to fight, and it slowly started to walk around the oval arena. Surprisingly, the very first attack from Isaac, who ran toward the Chimera and stabbed it in its knee fracturing it. The Chimera was no longer able to use his back right leg because of the wound. After the hit to its leg the Chimera spat a fire ball out of its goat head, and Isaac blocked it, he once again sacrificed his wooden shield. The crowd grew silent not expecting Isaac to battle this well.

Isaac lunged at the Chimera now striking it in the chest after blocking the fireball it had spit at him. The Chimera was then in major pain grunting on the ground. The crowd started cheering as the blood started spewing from the Chimeras chest causing the guards to run into the Royal Arena to drag the Chimera out of it. Isaac however, then passed out.

When he next woke he had a spear and shield forced into his hand. His body felt heavy from the new armor. Isaac realized what was happening as he was shoved for the fourth time into the arena. The loudest chant yet **"10, 9, 8, 7, 6, 5, 4, 3, 2, 1 BATTLE!"**

As the gate opened out came a massive **DRAGON!** At least 15 feet tall and 20 feet long adorned with crimson scales. Isaac jumped as he realized there was **BLOOD** on the scales! The smell was terrible, it smelled like a basket of spoiled milk coated, moldy cheese covered, gym shorts. Then it roared like a massive bear. The sound made Isaac shiver in pure fear. He turned to run, but then remembered there was nowhere to go. The arena was just a big hot, sandy, gray, oval. Tired of waiting the huge beast charged.

Quickly reacting, Isaac threw his spear at the firedrake (fire breathing dragon) stopping and stunning the beast. However, the spear shattered like a matchstick against its mighty body. There were mages that flew over the arena and kept the beast in check so that it would not fly away and so that it would continue to fight. Then the firedrake shot a blast of flame at Isaac who smartly rolled out of the way. Isaac survived, however, he had all hairs on his body singed off. As the dragon whirled around to face Isaac, he desperately threw his helmet at it, realizing armor wouldn't help him. Luckily for Isaac instead of hitting the indestructible scales, the helmet hit the dragon in the right eye, half blinding it.

The beast let out a huge roar which shook the entire arena and knocked down Isaac. In a panicked rage it dove- bombed toward Isaac hoping to crush him. Isaac whipped off all his armor *(boots, chest plate, and pants)* and heaved all of the items at the creature. The armor pieces did not seriously injure the creature, but it knocked it off its path, causing it to head-butt the ground and thereby stunning it. Isaac scurried away into a corner trying to think of a way to win. Then he had an idea, but had to get close to the monster for it to work.

The monster swung its spiky tail at Isaac only grazing

him, yet still knocking the wind out of Isaac. Then, it charged once again trying to eat Isaac. Isaac hurled his last piece of equipment that he had, his shield, into the dragon's mouth. The dragon stumbled back then tried to breathe fire making an explosion in its own mouth because the shield blocked the flame.

Isaac finally let his guard down and started to celebrate as blood spouted out of the creature's mouth. Then, **CHOMP!** There went the top half of Isaac. As the dragon died, its final action was to take Isaac with him.

(2 days later.) Everyone who knew Isaac was around his casket as he was buried. His brothers had to admit brute strength was not everything. The king stated that he wished he had made Isaac a soldier, instead of a gladiator. The town mourned for months, then went back to normal. That, is how the story of Isaac ends.

CHAPTER 3

Deep Blue

By: Lily Asbee

Last thing I remember I was on a yacht... My friends were throwing an end of the year party. I lived in West California, so I didn't have to travel far to get to the coast. I remember Ricky, my best friend was rocking the yacht by jumping to the beat of the music. It was the beginning of May, just a few days in, and I was excited to go on a road trip with a bunch of my friends.

I was sitting on the edge of the boat drinking sparkling cider, when suddenly... I see Mandy. She was the prettiest girl in school! I started to get nervous and jumpy at the sight of her. The yacht started to move with the big waves that were coming in. I lost grip as the yacht jostled around. I fell back. Apparently we weren't close to the shore anymore, we were so far I couldn't see the dock. But I didn't fully realize, Mandy had caught my attention. I barely knew what was happening. I tried to swim up but my long blonde hair got in the way, and I was blinded for a few seconds. I remember hearing "Dannie!" and then the yacht moved up and down once again, the front came up and the bottom came down. I was struck in the head so hard I passed out. I sank slowly into the ocean.

I awoke startled and afraid. I looked around me… I wasn't on land. I was on the bottom of the ocean. "How am I still alive?" I thought to myself. My head still hurt, but that didn't matter anymore. I swam up so my body was straight, almost like standing up. I was breathing, but how? I was in water, none of this made any sense. "Maybe I'm a merman! *looks at legs* Nope.". I had no clue what was going on but I had to get to the surface. But how? It was pitch black, and I could be anywhere right know! My feet left the freezing rocky sand. I swam up cautiously. It had got brighter, when I saw something… I looked at it for a minute. It was an Angler fish.

So nothing to be afraid of I thought. It swam closer, I was still looking at it fascinated. It had a light bulb like pod hanging from his head. Even though I had studied marine biology in high school, I still have no idea what they are called. It started swimming quicker towards me, when I realized how sharp its teeth were. I swam up as fast as I could. My dad had warned me about them, but in high school they said they were harmless. It bit my foot so bad I could feel chunks of flesh missing. Not so harmless huh Mr. Sam! I continued to swim as fast as I could, but inside I was screaming in agony. I had found some rocks as I came out of what looked like a trench. I hid behind them, but the Angler was long gone.

I came out slowly from behind the rocks. "AHHHH!" something was touching my foot. I kicked hard, but it was just a Blue Ringed Octopus. I let it stay on my uninjured leg for a while until it moved onto the corrals next to me. I looked at my open wound, it was stinging so badly, from the salt in the ocean, and the fact I had just got chunks ripped out of my foot. I sat on the rocks, thinking what had just happened in the past 24 hours. Or maybe it had been longer. I don't know, I'm just scared. I was just thinking as I moved my hand and felt something squishy. I looked over at what I was touching, and there behold… A gigantic Blue Sapphire Giant Squid. It was the most terrifying, yet gorgeous thing I had ever seen. Its blue gorgeous soft skin felt like nothing I had ever encountered.

They were the most endangered squid in the whole world. Again I don't know if I should be happy or scared. Its giant eye was closed, it was sleeping so peacefully. They were endangered for a reason. People hunt them because they are also the most dangerous marine animal in the world. They rip their prey so quickly and viciously, the animal usually doesn't notice until it's too late. I slowly took my hand of the beautiful creature. I almost got away when, the blood from my injured foot, went straight underneath its nose. Its huge eye slowly opened. I stay there terrified. I swam slowly to the small cave next to the squid, when the squid rapidly awoke. It made a huge shrieking sound that pierced my ears like a million needles. I swam as fast as I could to the cave but one of its huge tentacles hit me in the stomach like a sledge hammer. I sank slowly as the squid shrieked once again piercing my ears. Its tentacles hit me in the back and I heard a crack in my spine. I sank faster.

But somehow a Whale Shark came out of nowhere and distracted the huge squid. I tried to swim to the cave again, the squid had moved so I had a better chance of making it this time. I saw clownfish, blue tangs, and angelfish scatter as the squid shrieked. I swam as fast as I could to the rocky cave…. I made it. I was inside the freezing cold cave with huge gashes in me. My back wouldn't even allow me to make it straight, I could only hunch it.

The cave was filled with purple and pink crystals that reflected the little light coming from a hole at the top of the cave. It was gorgeous, unlike anything I had ever seen before. I was so amazed, luckily I was able to enjoy this because the pain in my foot had gone down. I was able to move around as if I was hoping on 1 foot. When suddenly I hoped on the wrong thing. I looked down to see what that squishy sensation was, I thought it was all in my head until they squealed. Thousands of baby Blue Sapphire squids! They may not be as big as the parent but they were just as dangerous. And they were all camouflaged onto the blue crystals I had been admiring. They were everywhere. On the walls, ceiling, floor, everywhere! They charged but I was able to get out in time. No wonder the big one was extremely aggressive, she was just protecting her babies. I held onto the corrals that were on the outside of the cave as I watched the baby squid come speeding out of the cave as if they were being shot out of a gun. Once they were out of sight, I swam to the nearest corral reef. The bright colored fish and corrals made me feel a little bit better about my day.

A couple hours had passed and I started to get hungry. I wondered about what to eat when I thought of raw fish. I mean I eat sushi all the time in school, home, pretty much anywhere. How different could it be? It's raw fish none the less. I looked for salmon, which of course I was. When I realized salmon don't live in the ocean. So I switched to the next fish I could find. I suddenly spotted a gorgeous white, yellow, and black crested angelfish.

I followed the fish until it stopped and I lunged at it. I grabbed it and forced it into my mouth. I could feel it squirming and the blood coming out. It was slimy and disgusting, nothing like sushi at all. But I had to eat something, I forced it down my throat. It took a few swallows to get it fully down, even then I could feel it still alive in my stomach. I would be better off eating a sea urchin.

It began to turn dark above the water, I had kept swimming and seeing if I was any closer to land, but it seemed as if I was getting further away. I had no concept of time but it was probably midnight by know. I floated above the water for a few minutes until I saw something, an island? A boat? I swam as fast as I could towards the object and I got so close I could touch it. I sat on the blue wet object, it was very bumpy and rocked know and then. I fell asleep on the big blue object, then woke up to a big "WHAAWHAAAWHAAAAAEEEEEEE!!!" I jumped up and fell into the cold water below me. I was sleeping on a rather comfortable blue whale. He whacked his mighty tail against the cold water, and swam away.

I was swimming the same direction of the whale for quite a while, when I started going the opposite direction, and I'm glad I did because that gave me a big head start for what was about to come. I suddenly heard the whale shrieking and screaming so loud you could hear it 5 miles away. I turned around and saw a big grey thing attacking it, I thought it was a great white for a minute but it was obviously much bigger than a great white when I looked at it from under water. It was huge, bigger than the sapphire squid I had seen before. It had 4 huge fins, all of them at least the size of me. It was murdering the whale right in front of me. I could see his huge teeth from just were I was, there where the biggest teeth I had ever seen in my lifetime. They were the size of my arms. It had huge spikes running from its head down to its huge slim tail. Then I realized what it was, a mosasaurus, they have been extinct for millions of years how is that possible? Maybe they have been hiding from humans for as long as they could to avoid possible extinction, but I doubt they were that smart. They were also the most feared and dangerous dino of their era, they killed everything in their sight. I slowly turned around and then bolted the other direction of the animal.

I thought I would escape the huge animal but as I turned around to see if I could still see the animal, and I couldn't. I did a little happy water dance as I turned around to see the most terrifying thing I had ever seen in my life. The huge monster of an animal was standing before me, huge teeth, spikes going from the head to the slim tail. Eyes that screamed of death and murder, black as the night they were. Grey skin that looked as if it was leather, blood stained tongue, with whale chunks wedged in between the teeth of yellow. Its huge body in a world of blue, never looked so beautiful. I stay there motionless in awe about everything this monster had. He open and closed his eyes but never lunged at me. We both just stood there as if we were afraid of each other. Scared to make the first move. He slowly opened his eyes one last time before he came close to me, we were in arms reach of each other, or in his case fins reach. I touched his spiky grey head as he closed his eyes.

Here we were, in the middle of a huge blue ocean surrounded by nothing except water. The giant creature backed up, opened his mouth and lunged at me. Then everything was black nothing but black.

I woke up to Ricky shaking me like an insane person. He kept asking if I was ok , I said "Yeah what happened to me?", "You drank too much champagne, and wiped out" Apparently when is saw Mandy I got nervous and started drinking champagne. Which I wasn't allowed to do since I'm under aged. But no one stopped me, not one of my closest friends had tried, in fact 1 Ricky said Mick one of my friends started drinking with me, and he got drunk and hurt himself pretty badly. I sat up because I was laying on the deck covered in champagne I had spilled. I got up and grabbed the bottle… I was in shock and almost dropped the bottle when I read the name, "DEEP BLUE CREATURES, BY MOSA SAPPHIRE" I nearly fell of the boat. As I went to throw the bottle away, I realized I was the only one on the boat, all my friends just left. I was alone again.

CHAPTER 4

Crushed

By: Zarmeena Azmat

After a 23 hour journey by plane, I am finally here. Pakistan. Yes! Pakistan. A burst of hot, humid air struck my face when I stepped out of the immigration lobby of the airport. We visit our grandparents every 2-3 years. It›s always very exciting for us, first the long plane ride with a lot of movies, games, unlimited coke and yummy food. Secondly visiting different transit airports every time. Dubai, Istanbul, Abu Dhabi and this time it was London.

We got into the car with 12 suitcases, 3 siblings, my mom and my grandfather. What are in those 12 suitcases, I really don't know. Off course we had to halt a taxi to carry our luggage to our grandparent's home. Life will be stress free now. No homework, no worries for next two months.

When I opened my eyes the next morning, I had a feeling of happiness, and I knew that something good was going to happen. Maybe my mom will buy me something from the new mall that opened, or we could go visit our cousins. As soon as I got dressed my mom called me for breakfast. When my mom sat down herself she told me that today we were going to the mall, not the new one because that was too far away. After breakfast I laced up my Converse and jumped into the car. Not kidding, I actually jumped onto the seat through the car window.

The only thing that I didn't like about the trip to the mall was my brother's side of the car window. It was open and since we were driving fast, my hair was blowing in my face. The cool breeze of the mall air conditioning made us nostalgic for our centrally air conditioned malls and homes of America. While exploring the shops I felt a minor headache. I didn't pay much attention to it, and I thought it is because the temperature was 90°F. My headache started getting worse and I couldn't ignore it anymore.

"Mom! My head really hurts" I said.

Maybe it was the look on my face that made her really worried.

"What happened Ayesha? Oh my God! You look so pale."

She hurried us to the food court, sat me down and rushed to get me a glass of water. Mom wanted me to eat, but I couldn't. I was feeling nauseous. My happiness had vanished and the trip back home was very painful.

After this trip headaches became a part of me and a normal thing. Some days I had minor headaches and some days really bad ones. I couldn't enjoy anything anymore. My cousins came, and left. I had to deprive myself from all fun. My mom concluded, "Headaches are because of severe heat." Worse of all, our supply of Children's Tylenol was running out.

My headaches were never leaving my head and I was still left with a whole month of holidays. My mom started searching for local neurologists and luckily we found one quick.

The weather was perfect outside. I felt the cool breeze on my face through the open window. That was a usual pattern of weather here in Islamabad. After two, three weeks of excruciating heat the clouds will come with rain. The week after that it will be very pleasant. As Islamabad lies under the Margalla Hills which are connected to Karakorum Mountain Ranges.

"Ayesha! Ayesha let's go play outside."

"It's cloudy with a chance of meatballs, no, no, with a chance of rain!"

My sister giggled, she has to make everything sound funny.

"No, my head hurts, don't bother me." I answered grumpily.

"Why on earth do you have headaches at the wrong times? Your headache is giving me a headache now."

"Mom, Fatima is bothering me."

"I am not."

"Yes you are."

"Stop you two!" My mom shouted in an angry voice.

"Okay, we are going to the park, you can stay home and mourn." Fatima exclaimed in a voice that she thought would make me jealous. "Poor you"

"Go away" I moaned.

"Ahh! Why me?"

The neurologist told my mom that migraine in kids is not just a bad headache. It›s a complicated neurological disease, with head pain and other symptoms, like nausea, vomiting, dizziness, sensitivity to touch, sound, light, and odors. Abdominal pain and mood changes can occur, too. Unfortunately, migraine is very common in children.

"Ayesha why are so quiet today? You were not even talking in the bus. Do you have headache? Did you take your medicine?"

Jacky was my only friend who knew about my headaches. She always kept two Tylenol with her at all times just in case I had a headache. The rest of my friends think that I suffer from mood swing, but like good friends they leave me alone.

We all got up for lunch in between the second period. I had a slight headache since I woke up. I was getting late for school, and forgot to take my migraine medicine. I couldn›t eat my lunch, because was feeling nauseated. I knew I would have to call my mom to bring the medicine. Otherwise, I won›t be able to concentrate in school.

It's been two years now since my migraine started. I saw a neurologist in Atlanta as well. He said the same thing as the Pakistani doctor, "I will have to live with it because it won't go away."

CHAPTER 5

Death's War

By: Jacob Ball

September 23, 1965:

Today, our government joined the war in Vietnam. I wish we could stop getting into wars. I am afraid that they will start drafting soon.

October 12, 1965:

Today is my son's eleventh birthday. I am so proud of the man he has grown to be. But with every good, comes a bad. I got a letter from the government saying I would be drafted on November first. It also said my Battalion. I will be a part of the One-hundred-tenth Battalion under Lieutenant Dan Taylor. I don't know if I should be excited or not.

November 1, 1965:

I can't believe I am going to a new place. Luckily, the base is only a couple of miles from my house. My wife and kids are scared. They fret that I might be killed in war. I hope they aren't too worried about me. I'm sure the army will take good care of me.

December 10, 1966:

The training has been intense. I have been forced to shave my head and get rid of all of my clothes. I was expected to only wear the provided military uniforms that barely fit. My friends and I have been treated like animals, we barely get sleep. It is just horrible. I can't stop thinking about my family.

February 16, 1966:

I just was notified that I will be shipped out in a month. I can barely work the gun that they gave us. In simulations, I always get wounded and die. I just hope the simulations won't become reality.

March 16, 1966:

I just landed in Vietnam. The only thing that is the same as the United States is the heat and the shrimp. I met Lieutenant Dan. I tried to salute him but he said, "Put your hand down! There could be assassins all around here who would love to kill a general." I put my hand down and went to my tent to unpack.

Junel 30, 1966:

Lieutenant Dan always had these "feelings" that this guy named Charlie was around. So, he would tell us to get down. And of course, we would. One day, it started raining, and it didn't stop. I learned this was called monsoon season.

September 29, 1966:

This is Dallas' friend, Cleveland. We were going

through a battle and Charlie showed up. They started killing us left and right. Then, bombs started going off. Dallas' left side was burned. Only Lieutenant Dan and I survived, but Lieutenant Dan's legs were gone. They lifted us out on a helicopter. I don't know how to tell his family that he got killed. I will give this notebook to his family so this will probably be the last entry.

Please return to Dallas' House (**** **** Road)

Phone Number (***-****)

CHAPTER 6

The Day my Dog got Loose (Again)!!!

By: Gabriel Brown

It was a beautiful, sunny day. My Mom, Dad, little brother, and I were ready to take Pepper for a stroll around the neighborhood. Who is Pepper you ask? She is my dog. She has beautiful brown eyes full of curiosity. Her tongue is always ready to lick anyone in her path.

Recently she has gotten free from my Mom's grip while walking her. And every time, she runs like she was in jail for thirty years and now was finally being set free. However, this time was different. This time the whole Brown Family was coming.

After putting her collar on, putting on the leash, and tightening it until only her hair could pass through the gap. We went on our way. The Sun shining down on everyone and everything.

"How was school yesterday," my Dad asked.

"It was okay," I responded.

"What does that mean."

"You don't expect me to say it was great because every Monday - Friday for 180 days I have to wake-up at…"

"At least you don't have as much homework as me," interrupted Sam.

Then out of the blue, a squirrel jumps onto the sidewalk right in front of our black lab. She spots the squirrel immediately. She bolts out of the leash like a bullet out of a gun. She runs like the wind chasing the squirrel into the woods and then silence. Absolute silence.

The next thing you know is the whole neighborhood waking up. Not from their alarms, but from four voices.

After a while we start walking up to our house and then walk inside worried about what will happen to her. Later, this noise of the trees rustling startles us and we bolt outside to see the commotion.

Their in our front yard is Pepper lying down with a squirrel in her mouth lifeless. My Dad comes to Pepper, picks her up, and carries, her with the dead squirrel in her mouth, inside. That day was an interesting day.

Pepper had her fair share of free time that day. My Mom says that she does not come back to us really early because she never runs free and want's to play a game of chase with us.

Although she can be a big pain in the butt she is our dog and we love her. We buried the squirrel later that day among the two baby birds, and 19 other squirrels she killed in her lifetime.

So that's the story of my dog getting loose. Again.

CHAPTER 7

Special Me

By: Anna Burnett

"Look at her shirt, it's so babyish!"

"I know and her hair, so 3 years ago!"

These are just some of the hushed whispers I hear as I walk through the hallways of my school. It's nothing new, you would think I'd be used to it by now but it still hurts. Let me introduce myself, hi my name is Harper Grey. I'm eight years old. I like to play outside, draw, play dress up, read (but sometimes it's hard for me) and any other normal 2nd grade hobby. One thing separates me, I'm special. The technical term is autistic, but I prefer special!

Every day is the same, I wake up, get ready, eat some food, and rush off to school. Mrs. Davison gets me off the bus and walks me to the classroom. I'm always so confused, I only have 10 kids in my class, but my sister has 29! I guess its ok, I like most of the kids in my class.

My best friend is Imani, she is my age too. She talks more than most kids in my class, but she hangs out with me in the playroom even though I don't talk. There are many different kids in my class. We have Tally, who loves to be active, she always plays on the swings. Jack, who is very quiet and is a very good reader. We also have Clea who always cries, I try not to talk to her, so she will not cry about what I said. Bo who talks too much (he gets in trouble a lot). Also, Naomi who loves to draw, she can draw horses really well! Dexter who is violent and sucks his thumb. Sage who is also violent, but not in a bad way, he takes Tae Kwan Do. Finally, Danny, he is always out so I don't know much about him except that he is loud. I think my class is cooler than most, because we are all special.

One day after a three-day weekend, the counselor came in with a group of kids, about 5th grade.

"Hi, everybody these kids are your new peer helpers! They will come in every Tuesday and Friday during recess and play with you!" Mrs. Johnson, the counselor, explained. We all kind of looked at each other not knowing whether to be happy or scared, nobody ever plays with us. Sage was so happy, he started showing off his karate moves. Everybody else started getting crazy as well. It was decided, we were happy! The counselor talked to the teacher some more and then said

"There will be one peer buddy for each child. We would have one day where all the peer buddies would come in and play with all the children. The teacher would watch and find out who works best with who!"

When that day came, I was so nervous. Would anyone want to play with me? All of the kids sat anxiously waiting for the peer buddies to come. When the 5th graders finally got there, we all went to the sensory room (some people call it the playroom, but that sounds babyish, so I call it the sensory room). I immediately went to the castle, (it is really a plastic house, but I like to think of it as a castle!) I sat there losing myself in my imagination, designing my castle. It would have big beautiful spiral stairs with chandeliers on my high ceilings. All the bed sheets as soft as velvet. I was 1,000,000 miles away when I heard a noise. I looked back and it was a 5th-grade girl.

"Hi, my name is Ava Howard."

I don't talk much, really only to my parents. I stared at her blankly wondering what to do next.
Ava scooted up next to me and started talking.

"This is a cool room, and this house reminds me of a castle!"

My eyes winded at the fact that she thought it was a castle too.

"Me too," I mumbled awkwardly not having talked in a few hours.

"Really, that's cool. I'm a pretty good drawer, I could draw your castle if you describe it to me."

I didn't know how to respond I was so happy. Before I could process my next response, Mrs. Davison called for the 5th graders.

"Think about it, OK!" Ava whispered before running off.

On the bus ride home, Imani was talking about how her soon-to-be buddy was so cool, and how she helped her play on the swing. She talks to me a lot even though I don't respond. She knows I'm listening. I really wanted to tell her how my soon-to-be buddy (I hope) was going to draw me my castle, and how cool she was but I didn't think she would understand. When it was my stop, my parents helped me get off the bus and go to my house. My parents didn't understand why I was so excited. I didn't have a very good vocabulary so it was hard to explain.

"School fun, I have buddy who draw a castle" I mumbled as specific as possible.

"You made a new friend!" mom cheered.

"She likes to draw," dad added.

I tried to explain she was my soon-to-be peer buddy, but they didn't understand. I just nodded after a few failed attempts and ran upstairs. When I passed my sister's room she was busy doing homework, I am very lucky I never have homework! I ran to my room while I waited for my afternoon snack, I started telling my fish Opie all about school.

"Knock knock, did someone order cheese and crackers?"

My dad came in and put the snack down.

"Are you ready, which story today?"

Every day after school while I'm eating my snack Dad read me a book. Sometimes he let me try to read a page!

I pointed to a book with a gold spine and little people on the front, the name was "Riddles Riddles A to Z"

"Okay, here we go-"

Before he said the first word Mom called him, they were always talking under their breath and quickly stopping when I came into the room. Mom is always on the phone and dad always looking at pamphlets.

"Hold on just a moment sweetie I have to go help your mom"

I nodded okay but really felt betrayed. As he rushed downstairs I crept to the landing to try to eavesdrop.

"Honey, they will call, it takes a long time."

"I know but, it is taking too long."

My heart stopped when I realized what they were talking about. It all made sense, the long calls and the pamphlets. They were talking about sending me away for the summer. To one of those " I -can't-deal-with-my-autistic-kid-this-summer" escape for parents. I ran to my room and slammed the door shut. The cheese and crackers stood untouched. My parents started coming up.

"Sweetie, what's wrong?" My dad asked.

"Did you hear us talking? It's not that bad." Mom added.

Not that bad? I thought. Parents abandoning their children! Not that bad? To a camp in the middle of who knows where? Not that bad?

They walked in with sympathetic faces, ready to explain to me, but I wasn't ready to listen.

"A baby is not that bad" mom explained.

I jerked my head out of the pillow where I had stuffed it. A what is not what!?

"A what?" I mumbled.

"A baby, that is what we were talking about, wasn't that what you were upset about?" mom asked questioningly.

Relief flooded my body when I realized I wasn't being sent away. After my parents explained that they were adopting a baby and they were waiting for a call to hear the news, the dread came back. I didn't want another sibling. My parents wanted me to help name it, and all I could think about was the fact I would not be the youngest of two but instead the middle of three. I blurted out the name I was going to name my child one day, Felicity.

"What a great idea!" mom shouted.

"Better than Riley," Dad added.

No, no, no I thought. That name is mine. I didn't have the nerve to tell them that. When they left, I fell into a deep sleep dreaming about Felicity. Who knows which one.

The next day at school I could hardly focus in music I was so excited about the peer buddies coming., I even forgot about the baby. When we got back to the class the peer buddies were already there.

"OK, when I call your name, go over to the first child in line!" Mrs. Davison called out.

The counselor put us in a line. I was the last person, Bo was the first.

"Here we go, Lily, Toby, Dory, Gabe, Jake, Riley,"

I laughed a little at that one remembering what dad said about Riley.

"Anna, Jordan,'

This was it, who would by my peer buddy, Ava, or some random kid?

"Ava, and David!" Mrs. Davison concluded.

I felt like all the happiness just got squeezed out of my body. Ava went to Tally, not me. I got the kid who was absent the other day!

"I'll let you talk for a few minutes, then we will go to the sensory room," The teacher said with a warm smile.

"Hi, my name is David. What's yours?" he said happily.

It's not that I didn't want to answer, I couldn't. I was shocked and sad. I lost my voice. I looked over at Tally happily talking to Ava.

"Um, so do you like to play?" David asked awkwardly sensing the fact I didn't want him.

After a few unanswered questions, we went into the sensory room. I ran to the castle, wishing I could take it home with me when David walked in. He had a hard time getting in, he was bigger than me or Ava. He finally stopped half way in.

"So, you like this place?"

I saw Ava drawing Tally playing on the swings. I was so sad. The entire time I stayed put. Halfway through David ran off to go play with other kids. I started crying. The teacher came in and asked where my buddy was. I pointed to David through the window.

"That's not your buddy, is it?" Mrs. Davison asked questioningly.

She ran to get her paper and came back saying that Ava was supposed to be mine and David was supposed to be Tally's! I was so happy, but felt bad for Tally. Mrs. Davison pulled David and Ava aside telling them about the mix-up. David looked relieved. Ava perked up a bit too! We had to leave after that. On the bus, Imani told me she got her buddy so everything was good. When I got home, I told Opie about my day because there was no story because of the baby...again. I practiced my speaking for Ava. I talked about my castle and my family. It took a long time to say it all good, but I had nothing else to do. At dinner, my parents gave us the big news- our baby brother would come home on Friday! I was happy it was a boy, not a girl.

"We are naming him James, " mom exclaimed.

We talked about him all night. The next day at school, we had P.E. I HATE P.E. I can't run very fast so it's embarrassing, especially with the other 2nd graders in there too. I was squirmy all through school waiting for Ava to come. When she did I was so happy!

"Hey Harper!" Ava exclaimed.

She had a drawing pad in hand ready.

"Castle!" I said, meaning for it to be a question.

"Yes, I brought my stuff!"

"It's big and tall windows pretty!" I started

"Whoa, whoa, whoa, slow down" Ava laughed.

The rest of the time we talked and drew. I was so excited to show my parents my castle. When Ava left, I told the teacher all about my castle. She was so happy I was talking! The rest of the week was the same. We talked a lot. By Friday I had a huge vocabulary! (bigger than before but not as big as Ava's). My parents loved how I talked. On the way home I forgot about James so I ran into the house almost knocking his crib over.

"Harper, Stop right now!" Dad yelled.

Dad had never yelled at me before. I lost all my brand new words and ran to my room. I dropped my note from the teacher while running. Mom came in and explained how things were going to be different now. I was not happy over the weekend. James kept taking time that should have been mine. Mom and dad didn't seem to care. He was a pain. Dad stopped reading to me all together. I told Ava these things and she said to talk to him, but I just couldn't. It was too hard for me. The only thing I liked any more was Ava. The only time I really talked was when she came. She even got permission to come almost everyday! I was so happy and it kept me from being sad about James.

The rest of the year I got smarter and better at talking. I took a test and might be moved to a bigger classroom next year! My teacher wrote mom and dad another note and they were so proud. They took me out to dinner, Just me! No James! I had to write a paper to tell them my story, so I did all about Ava and me. James got better as he got bigger, so mom and dad were able to spend more time with me, dad even started reading to me again! Imani and I have talks now. We really grew our friendship. I pull out to go to some classes now with her. This chapter of my life may be over but I can't wait to start a new chapter!

"Harper, time to go!"

Oh, I got to go! See ya later!

CHAPTER 8

The Keepers of Nightingael

By: Emma Busboom and Erin Eakin

Wind swept through the Kingdom of Nightingael, bringing a spell of calamity along with it. Disaster was about to strike in the heart of their believably oh-so stable empire. With all the ignorant and credulous royal prats roaming around the palace, it is a wonder the dragon keepers hadn't targeted the realm hitherto. Aspen Shadowthorn, an elf bystander, is determined to protect the provinces from all the malevolent sorcerers the idle wellborn's ignore. Her outgoing crony, Annalise Arrowbrook, intends to aid her and protect their birthplace from the silent predators and magical threats that loom nearby. But Aspen and Annalise aren't your ordinary pals.

Aspen has the power to wield fire, ice, and Earth, while Annalise has the power to control storms and can read all living things thoughts. Together, the duo have the potential to change history. They have already saved the kingdom from countless creatures such as goblins and trolls, but the king would never know it was *them* who saved the royal clotpoles from disaster. This was because all the wardens of the elements from the elders were supposedly cast out of Nightingael because they were viewed as a threat, therefore the females had no choice but to conceal their gifts. But nothing could prepare them for the egregious tasks and onuses ahead of them.

It all started with the two girls riding their masculine horses. Everyday, they rode and had pretend races. They could never enter in real races because they check your background and status, and they did *not* want people knowing about their powers. They would have been sent to the dungeons and executed if anyone found out.

"Are horse races really a necessary part of our day?" Aspen huffed quizzically.

"We need to keep active and stay felicitous just in case…" Annalise retorted.

"In case of *what*? Honestly, an orc isn't going to jump out of the bushes and doo us" ,Aspen scoffed as she cleared the roots along the path so the horses wouldn't trip. Annalise rolled her eyes stubbornly, but smiled at her friend. Aspen heaved an annoyed sigh and gave in. They continued along the trail and stopped at their usual resting place for a picnic before the course.

Annalise had prepared cheese and pickled herring sandwiches with a heap of pottage poured on top for lunch. Aspen picked at her food; she had no appetite.

"Aspen, your food isn't a fire so quit prodding at-", Annalise started. But just then, the ground started to rumble. The two girls were dumbfounded and flummoxed about what was happening and what had caused the shudder. The compacted Earth was trembling like the lower class citizens clothes when they billowed in the wind to dry. Nevertheless, they acted swiftly. They stood up, glanced at each other, and hopped onto their horses.

With a quick click of their tongues, the horses darted back into town obedieantly. That's when Aspen spotted it. Zaygoiphyth. Zaygoiphyth is the most menacing dragon in the whole realm. It's fiery breath could burn a whole kingdom down. Bestriding on the monster's spikey back was Zephyr Neige, Annalise could see his piercing blue eyes even from afar, his black wispy hair blowing back in the wind, and worst of all, the thin wicked smile that was plastered on his pale face.

Screams of children and adults could be heard around the two girls. Annalise's face turned bright red,

"That blundering swine! He never should've come here!"

Just as she finished her insult, the jagged tail of the dragon swung around, ripped Aspen's trousers and cut her knee open and sent Annalise flying into a cottage. Aspen grimaced in pain. Annalise attempted to stay awake, but the powerful blow was too much for her; she fell unconscious next to the small wooden residence.

Zaygoiphyth landed smoothly onto the ground and Zephyr slid off of the monster's scaly back.

"Well, well, well if it isn't the magical duo", he said with a laugh. Aspen glared up at him, holding her knee. He let out a little chuckle as he observed his surroundings.

"What do you want Zephyr?", Aspen questioned testily.

"What's the fun in telling you my plans?" He pondered. She continued scowling.

"But if you insist, I plan to conquer this kingdom and make it my own. Guess what? There will be no one to stop me, not even you...", he remarked putting the gaunt smile back on his face.

"What makes you think Annalise and I are going to let you conquer the kingdom?", she expressed.

"Oh little elf, my Zaygoiphyth is capable of stopping anyone, even people with magic", he threatened. Aspen stayed silent, not knowing what to say or do.

"And you two little power freaks are helpless", Zephyr added with a whisper. She turned to see Annalise laying on the ground, inert. Aspen stood up, and felt shivers run down her spine due to the trickling feeling of a runnel of blood forming a path down her kneecap. They stared at each other straight in the face, unmoving. After a long while of glaring, he sighed and snapped his fingers, Zaygoipyth drew his fiery breath and sent the lodge bursting into scorching flames.

"That was just a warning, next time you see me, villages will be burnt to a crisp. If your king Ivon Firay refuses to give up this empire, innocent people will die!", Zephyr hissed, turning his eyes away from Aspen and crawling back up Zaygoipyth's back.

She realized that Annalise was laying next to the flaming cabin. Aspen stumbled towards the cottage, scouring for the immobile Annalise. Tears were streaming down her face. What if she had lost her friend? Would it be her fault?, she thought. Ignoring the pain from her knee and splitting the flames apart with her powers, she desperately searched to save her cohort.

Finally she spotted her storm controlling friend.

"Annalise!" She said hoarsely dragging her out of the flames.

Annalise had ashes covering her arms and face, she wasn't as close to the fire as Aspen had thought. Aspen's knee throbbed. She shook her companion,

"Wake up! Please just wake up!"

The blaze died down and Aspen was able to find a bucket of water. She dumped the transparent liquid onto Annalise, she could see her eyes opening slowly.

"Annalise! You're awake!" She said.

"Agh my head, what happened?" She wondered.

"Zephyr came with Zaygoiphyth. We got struck with the dragon's tail, you went flying and got knocked unconscious. My knee was sliced open, then Zephyr told me that he wants to conquer Nightingael-" Aspen stopped once she saw Annalise wave her hands.

"Woah! Well Aspen, I've never heard you say that many words at once before; I love the enthusiasm to tell me all of this, but slow down a bit so I can understand you." Annalise said.

"I'm just really nervous. What are we going to do?", She questioned.

"Which direction did he fly off?", Her friend wondered.

"Northwest…."

"Alright, whatever he is going to do we *need* to stop him. We must be prepared. We must fight back! It is imperative we find a way to discreetly warn the king to arm his men." , Annalise said determinedly.

"He's never going to believe us, even if he saw the dragon. It's the king we're talking about. The foolish and power hungry menace is blind to everyone and everything but himself!", Aspen replied hopelessly, the fire in her eyes flickering out. Annalise heaved an irritated sigh.

"Looks like we're on our own" she announced.

"We need to follow him and stop Zephyr in his tracks" Aspen planned. They nodded to each other and mounted their steeds, Aspen was cautious about her knee while hopping onto hers. Now, they were heading into dangerous territory. Now, they would have to be careful. Now, they would need to use magic. Now, was their time to save Nightingael. They clicked their tongues, and once more the horses darted into the Mockingbird forest. Leaves crunched under the stallion's hooves as they rode through the dull timberland. The duo finally halted and scouted out a camping area. Aspen gathered wood and used her powers to ignite a fire. Annalise was getting ready to place down their bedrolls until there was a loud *crunch* that echoed through the woods.

"What was that?" Annalise asked in a whisper. Aspen placed her finger on her lips to signal Annalise to be quiet.

Then a sudden movement came sweeping in and flipped Aspen over onto her back. Annalise felt a hard blow come to her back which caused her to collapse. Aspen struggled to stand and could feel a sharp pain in her knee. However, determined to find out who was causing this, she stood up. A figure jumped up in front of her and she kicked it as hard as she could.

Annalise grabbed the figure that was standing behind her and twisted its wrist, turning it over onto its back. She held down its shoulders and legs to keep it from moving. Then, slowly, she took off its woven hood. The person was revealed to have hair containing a medley of different variations of the color burnt sienna and radiant chestnut streaks. Along with intense gray eyes with his midnight black, slightly enlarged pupil. He looked to be around their age, and had a look of pain on his face.

"Get off of me!" he gasped, his hand struggling to move Annalise's navy hood from her head. Though she succeeded in keeping his rather strong hand in place, the effort jolted her cloak out of its position in blocking her face.

Annalise looked over at Aspen for help, but could see her pinned down by another man, who was removing her cream colored hood.

"Get off! What in the WORLD do you think you are doing!?", Aspen shrieked, feeling a sharp pain in her patella, looking into the depths of her intruders electrifying green eyes, with a dark green lining the iris, and blond hair with highlights of brown. He looked the about the age of Aspen. She grimaced in pain; the attacker realized this was due to him crushing her wrist into the hardened dirt, and relinquished his grip quickly. He turned his direction to his partner and saw that he was talking to the girl that was pressing him to the ground.

"Oh, well, ma'am, if you will accept my deepest of apologies. Sometimes we get raiders in these parts of the Mockingbird's, and we feel like it is our duty to stop whatever lying cheat that comes our way...miss, could you please, um, remove your binding hands?". The male who looked to be around 17 pleaded with Annalise, who swiftly and smoothly pulled her body from above his, locking him into an awkward hug as she lifted him off the ground.

"What is your name?!" Annalise asked slowly.

"My name is Mason Lockwood", he replied with a slight smile.

"And yours is-?"

"Annalise Arrowbrook", she said, narrowing her eyes, not wanting to assumingly and too easily trust these strangers.

Aspen's aggressor took her hand and pulled her up.

"Are you alright?" the man questioned worriedly. Aspen shook her head, falling back down to the ground. However before she fell, the man moved his arm and snatched her back to keep her from collapsing.

"What is your name?" He asked.

"Aspen Shadowthorn" she answered timidly.

Aspen, still cradled in the man's arms, looked over at Annalise, who was giving a rather long handshake to her latest victim.

"He really is sincere, you know. His name is Nixon Frostfall and him and Mason are from the outer province of Ivarhold in Nightingael.", Annalise retorted knowingly. The boys stared wide-eyed at the knowledge that spouted from the mind reading mage. The boy Annalise identified as Nixon quickly let go of Aspen, and she found her footing again with the aid of a nearby Elm tree.

"How did you-?" he questioned.

"Annalise you shouldn't have said that" Aspen said in between clenched teeth.

"You have magic...do you?" Nixon interrogated. Annalise shook her head trying to deny it, fury flaming in her knowing blue greyish eyes. Mason turned towards Aspen and asked,

"And do you have magic as well?" He spent no time questioning the girls; he knew it was true.

"Y-yes", she answered, looking down in shame. Nixon once again clutched Aspen's hand and lifted her off the dry leaves, noticing her bloody knee. He helped her over to the fire. He placed his hand over the gash and there was a slight glow. Once he had removed his hand Aspen's knee was fully healed. She sat there in shock.

"You have magic too..." she mumbled, still unsure of him. He gave a slight nod then smiled. Annalise and Mason came and sat by the fire.

"Mason, do you have any powers?" Annalise questioned. He looked at the ground then his body transformed into a furry brown wolf.

"A shapeshifter!" Annalise cheered. Mason morphed back into his regular form and continued staring at the ground.

"Nixon and I ran away from Ivarhold, an outer province of Nightingael, because people discovered our powers. We escaped before they could do anything to us, but now we are living on the run. But enough about us, what's your story?", Mason asked.

Aspen stayed silent; she didn't like talking to people she didn't know that well. Plus, she didn't trust the two boys.

"Well Aspen and I have lived in Nightingael for our whole lives. We've managed to keep our powers a secret. Anytime Nightingael was in trouble, we would be the ones to save the kingdom, but no one knows that. Then today, Zephyr came with his dragon Zaygoiphyth and threatened the kingdom. He flew northwest, so we are planning to stop him in his tracks" Annalise explained.

"Just the two of you? Defeat Zephyr?" Mason snorted. Aspen glared at him, while Nixon shook his head.

"I don't doubt your power, but it will be hard to stop this man. We'll join you!", Nixon assured. Annalise

looked at Aspen, who sat up a little bit. Aspen started to trust this strange man.

"Do you have any other powers...besides your healing abilities?" Aspen quizzed, mumbling a little. Nixon turned his attention towards a stick and the piece of wood started to float in the air.

"Hmm telekinesis..." she said. She looked at Annalise who rolled her eyes.

"Fine you can join us...but I will be watching your thoughts." she huffed. Nixon nodded along with Mason.

"We should get some rest," Aspen suggested. There was a murmur of agreement, then Nixon and Mason set up their sleeping area. The fire died down as everyone fell asleep. Aspen tossed and turned, then finally got up and sat in the damp grass gazing at the stars. She was uneasy, Aspen found it hard to sleep when she was nervous. The cool air brushed across her cheeks, followed by a long sigh. She wrapped her arms around her legs, shivering a bit.

"Can't sleep?" She heard a voice say. She turned her head to see Nixon standing a few feet from where she struggled to drift off. Aspen shrugged her shoulders and let him slip into the patch of grass next to her.

"So, have you ever encountered Zephyr before?", Aspen conversed quietly after a long and, rather uncomfortable silence. Nixon looked at the ground.

"He flew into our old town...it was disastrous to say the least. All I could see was red and orange. Flames and screams from innocent people shot up like flares every few paces. My parents were both burned alive. I can still hear their pleading cries in my nightmares. Some

57

were murdered by Zephyr himself. He is a creature of the very maleficent four corners of the Earth. You can't mess around with him", Nixon stammered, a distance look moving like a cold front across his lucid face. Aspen placed her cold hand on his warm palm, feeling his presence and his pain.

"I'm sorry Nixon" she whispered, imagining everything and everyone she loved reduced to cinder.

"There was nothing you or anyone else could have done, Aspen. That is why we need to cut off this man, if I can even call him a human, in his tracks: because if he makes it back into Nightingael...I'm afraid your kingdom is beyond saving." he explained. Aspen looked away.

"There is still hope Nixon. We may struggle, but I know with the four of us, we will save Nightingael", she proclaimed warily, turning her attention back to the stars. Her eyes began to close, she finally felt the urge to sleep. Her head absentmindedly fell on Nixon's shoulder as she drifted to sleep.

She awoke to sound of camp being packed up. Her head was still placed on Nixon's shoulder. Aspen shot up.

"Did you sit here the whole night?" she questioned. Nixon nodded.

"I didn't want to wake you", he replied. Aspen rolled her eyes playfully, but still smiled as she walked over to Mason and Annalise. She helped them load their supplies onto the horses. The four hopped onto their equestrians, and began to trot along the path in the Mockingbird woods. The forest was dark and cold. Winds stabbed at

Annalise's cheeks like shards of ice piercing her, while flurries began to fall from the sky. Nature could be painful like the subzero wind, or beautiful like the petite snowflakes drifting down.

"What exactly are we looking for?", Mason asked after almost a half an hour of silence.

"Zephyr. We saw him fly off on Zaygoiphyth, heading northwest. It is well known he loves to reside there in caves. Our best guess is looking in the Evergreen mountains", Aspen murmured.

They continued along the lengthy pathway for another hour in virtual silence until they reached a clearing in the forest. A small village sat on the east side of a thin river slicing through the trees. All of the cottages were eerily empty, and what seemed to be scorch marks scarred the oaks surrounding the town.

"Aspen...we were too late for these people...Zephyr must be striking the concealed hamlets first!" Annalise cried. The four dismounted off of their horses Aspen looked down at her hands; not saying a word. Trying to evade a guilty look, Nixon slowly wandered over to, what looked like, was an apothecary.

"This is why, this is why we quarrell with corrupt and wicked forces. *THIS IS WHY*! For now, it would be wise to take refuge here. But let this serve as a reminder; don't mess with these beasts, these intruders, these barbarians. I know the inhabitants of this village are past the point of redemption,, but if we collaborate, we will be the downfall of these brutes. As a result, protecting Nightingael.",

Nixon said, with a note of leadership creeping into his tone.

Aspen scoured around the area then found a body of what looked to be a small child. Tears filled her eyes and ran down her cheeks like a waterfall. It appeared that the juvenile had perished do to blood force trauma, and she had strips of flesh missing from her from her miniscule body. Next to the child, a small doll was laying in dried leaves, which was covered in putrid ashes. She looked away, pulled on her hood to hide her face, then walked off next to her horse.

"Should we search for survivors?" Annalise inquired.

"Don't you see?! There are no survivors, they're all dead! We can run but we cannot hide! This is Zaygoiphyth in action!", Aspen choked.

"Everyone. We should start collecting resources for our stay here. The time for mourning has passed. At some point, you must understand that bad things happen to good people.", Mason declared, wiping a small tear forming a stream of salty, sticky liquid down his face.

"We aren't staying here, we need to continue, Zephyr might do something like this again, Mason. If we stay here and take our time, there will be no hope for Nightingael." Nixon argued. Aspen nodded her head in agreement; still not saying a word.

"Then let's meet in the middle; we travel till nightfall. Then, we rest. We will just get ourselves killed if we attempt to fight Zephyr while exhausted." Annalise suggested.

"You're a coward, Annalise, we are a strong enough group.", Aspen scowled, glaring all the while.

"Aspen! You don't understand! We will be useless if we battle while falling asleep!", a small rain cloud appeared over the group's heads as Annalise became impatient.

They argued for a few minutes more, and decided they would rest for but an hour every six hours to be prepared. Aspen pulled her hood farther down to completely shroud her features.

"Aspen! Come with me to gather supplies. You need some time away from these people before we all slaughter each other. We meet back in half an hour to continue our trek.", Nixon requested. Aspen followed Nixon and helped him collect firewood. Thoughts of the dead child flashed in her mind. What if everyone in Nightingael had been butchered viciously like that child had? She shook her head to clear the shadowy thought from her brain.

Nixon looked over Aspen and gave her a smile to assure that she was alright. However, her face didn't seem to be smiling back. After they picked up enough fire wood, they strolled back to the scorched town.

Annalise and Mason stood by the stream, each holding a sharp stick. They were hoping to have fish for dinner; all of them had starved from the past events. Annalise saw a rather large brown fish gliding through the water, she jabbed her stick into the water and saw blood fill a small area of blue water.

"Nice catch!", Mason praised, catching a fish of his own. They wandered back to the ruined village holding several fish they had caught.

"I think we've got all the supplies we need" Nixon said. They wrapped up the fish in a small piece of cloth, put all the supplies in a satchel, and jumped onto their horses once more. Aspen stayed taciturn during the ride farther into the woods. Annalise came to an abrupt stop.

"There is a cave here, maybe we could build a fire and sleep in there" she suggested. There was a murmur of agreement from the two boys, still no noise from Aspen. The cave was frigid and was filled with the sounds of supplies being unloaded. The firewood was propped up, and with a flick of Aspen's fingers, the fire ignited. Mason held four fish over the fire to cook them. Once he was done, the fish were cut up into equal pieces for the group. They finished their meal, then drifted to sleep on their bedrolls.

Aspen was restless, many thoughts raced through her mind. Suddenly she heard a strange noise, like something sliding on the stone ground. She stood up swiftly and silently, being cautious not to wake anyone. As she descended further into the dark cave, whispers were fluttering in her ear. Finally she collided with a large object that felt to be scaly. She stumbled back and saw red eyes getting taller and taller. It was Zaygoiphyth. A cold, bony hand crept up onto her shoulder. Zephyr. She felt shivers run down her spine, like a thousand spiders crawling down her back.

"Get away from me" she threatened. However, the strong tail of Zaygoiphyth struck her right in the head.

She fell unconscious right in front of the monstrous dragon.

Annalise awoke to a ray of sunshine seeping through a crack in the cavern. She looked around at her friends, then noticed that Aspen was missing.

"Aspen?!" she cried, awakening the boys.

"Huh?" Nixon groaned.

"Aspen! She's missing!" she continued panicking. As she looked out of the grotto she saw that Aspen's horse was still tied to a nearby tree.

"She couldn't have run off! Her horse is still there!" Mason assured. Annalise shook her head, frantically standing up. The other two stood up as well.

"I'm sure she's fine, Annalise. She may have gone on a walk.", Mason said, trying to calm her down. Annalise shook her head.

"Aspen doesn't just go on walks. She always wants to be isolated in a room, not outside.", Annalise retorted. They sat in silence, thinking. The one chilling thing that broke the silence was a deep, nasty laugh. Annalise spun around to see Zephyr Neige smiling.

"Zephyr!", Annalise said stiffly, shooting him a glare. Nixon and Mason straightened their shoulders.

"Ah I see you've made some...friends...", he pointed out. Annalise could read everything he was thinking.

"What did you do to Aspen?" Annalise asked sternly. His face seemed calm, it was clear he wasn't surprised that Annalise had read his thoughts.

"Oh, the little elf? She wandered too far into the cave, she bumped into Zaygoiphyth. I didn't want her warning you that I was here, she's safe...under my watch."

"We can rescue her then!", Nixon hollered defiantly.

"Unfortunately, you cannot save her. You plan to stop me from conquering Nightingael, but there is one major setback; Aspen. If you try to stop me, she will die in cold blood", he terrorized. The three of their faces became dark. Once again, the same sinful laugh echoed through the hollow stone.

"I know you plan to fly into the central province in our kingdom in three days eve. You cannot deceive us. Try as you might, we will rise." Annalise's icy tone echoed around the profound cave, like someone trying desperately to get out of a mirrored maze. Her eyes glittered with all the loathing and hate she had been holding against the gangly man before her, along with the guilt and sorrow of her best friend's disappearance.

"Hmm, well, let's see about that...". His grotesque mouth was wrought into a gnarled smile as he leapt over the side of a brink on a rather large and bloodcurdling cliff that would give any child nightmares. This was not an act of unwillingness to live, however. Zaygoiphyth swept up and caught Zephyr squarely on his back.

The group was speechless. What could they really do against a powerful sorcerer aided with a gobsmacking dragon? They decided to practice collaborating and using their dynamisms all day and night until they rescued Aspen. What the naive Neige didn't realize was that the sly Annalise had lied about what Zephyr's plan was. She had said that to put him off his guard and let the true disposition slip in his mind. It had worked.

At a fleeting glance, Annalise had read that Zephyr intended to leave in two days morn, and he had fully believed Annalise truly thought that three days eve was his estimated time of departure. This worked out marvelously for the three present vigilantes. Annalise practiced creating jagged spears of hail, while secretly reading the flirtatious comments about her on Mason's mind while he practiced trying to control his movements when he morphed his body into a dragon. Nixon, however, was practicing telepathically moving rocks into a pile near him. He found himself shattering some rocks because of his anger, he wanted Aspen to be safe.He wanted Nightingael to be safe. One fit of anger caused him to hit Mason on the head with a rock.

In the morning, Mason turned into a bird and fly to get their breakfast. He ate quickly, then morphed into a bat to mask his presence in case he ran into Zephyr, then looked for Aspen.

"No luck…", Mason sighed warily when he got back.

"We train and then look again. We can't leave her in the mercy of some disturbed guy.", Nixon persisted

Meanwhile, Aspen tugged on the restraints that were holding her back. She wanted to escape, she wanted to see her friends, she wanted to protect her birthplace.

"You beastly creature! It is so inhumane of you to keep me here like an animal! Where is your pride!", Aspen sneered, centering her thoughts on Nixon...oh how she needed his telekinesis now to knock Zephyr out for a little bit...and Mason...he could turn into a spider or something to pick the locks and knots… and Annalise...oh how she wanted her cause a storm strong enough to kill Zephyr and Zaygoiphyth. She then remembered she had ice powers. She could freeze the chains and break them off of her wrists. Aspen would have to wait until Zephyr wasn't paying any attention to her, or when he was napping.

She waited patiently in the cave to enact her plan, while her acquaintances grew impatient.

"I can't wait anymore! I miss my friend! I'm going after her. We are going to fight Zephyr and Zaygoiphyth once and for all and save Aspen, along with Nightingael. Come with me right now or stay. I'm done. Take it or leave it." Annalise blurted.

"I'm coming with you. I would follow her to the end of the Earth if I thought she was in danger." Nixon's green eyes were watering slightly as he walked over to Annalise.

"I know she is important to you guys, and I know I have only known her for a short time, but she seems wonderful and I understand we need Aspen. So let's do this.", Mason retorted grimly. So the three set off on search of the one who completed their quartet.

Back in the cave, Aspen waited enduringly. Zephyr had fallen asleep against his pet dragon. She wanted to make sure he was in a deep enough sleep to not be awoken by a certain level of noise; she didn't know how loud this would be, or if it would even work. She created frost that covered her fingers, and soon enough, the chains were covered in ice. She could hear the snapping of the steel. Aspen tugged on them harder and they came out of the wall, broken free of her raw wrists. Moonlight helped Aspen find her way out of the chilling cave. A strong wind pushed at her face, making her breaths jagged, but still she looked for her buddies.

Farther in the mountains Nixon, Mason, and Annalise bolted across the trails on their horses with determination, they desperately wanted to save their friend, who was just a little bit more to a certain Nixon. Finally, the crowd started to sense a certain pulse in the air. Mason predicted it could be the dragon breathing.

As they neared the sound, they started to see a sliver of a scaly tail poking through an opening in a cavern.

"Zaygoiphyth…!", Annalise said breathlessly into the darkness with a mix of horror and relief, but to many shushes by the boys, she lowered her tone and said,

"This must be where they are keeping Aspen."

"I sure hope so…", Nixon replied anxiously.

They crept as little caterpillars scampering away from the large human hands. As they rounded the curve, they saw the infamous body of the giant dragon looming over a seemingly insignificant and puny human, but the experienced sorcerers knew better.

"Where is Aspen!", Nixon whisper screamed impatiently.

"Calm down, calm down we'll find her!", Mason reassured soothingly. While the crew starting silently searching the cave as quickly as they could possibly go. Just when they were about to give up on the idea that Aspen could possibly be in there, there was a tiny cough that came from behind them, Aspen stood there shivering in the cimmerian cave. Their faces lit up.

"Aspen!" Annalise whispered happily.

"Annalise!". She ran to her friend and embraced her like there was no tomorrow.

"Annalise I escaped an hour ago! I've been looking for you guys!", she stammered.

"I'd hoped you guys would come back here to find me, so I came back here when I saw that camp was empty." She smiled warmly towards Nixon.

"We are so glad you are safe!". He beamed back at her with adoration.

But just then, Zephyr started to stir.

"Shhhh!", Mason interjected, but it was too late. They were out of time. The team quickly spread out. Annalise was the first to react. She sent powerful gusts of wind towards Zephyr's figure, sending him flying into a stone pillar. If he wasn't already awake, he was now.

"Guys hurry he is starting to think we are here! Act fast!", Annalise cried.

Mason instantaneously turned into a dragon, and met Zaygoiphyth. It was battle time. Aspen was in the process of creating an arsenal of ice spears to throw at Zephyr as a distraction, while Nixon was concentrating with all of his brainpower on moving an elephantine boulder overhead the arousing diabolical dragon. Zephyr barely had time to process what was going on before he was being pelted with makeshift ice javelins, petrifying winds and hail, and the realization that his beloved Zaygoiphyth was fairly even in comparison to the fraudulent Mason dragon and the strength Nixon could behold using his telekinesis.

The assault was in full swing. It soon became obvious that the petty Zephyr Neige was no match for the four of them. Annalise kept her tornado bouts in full swing, while Aspen bombarded their adversary with ice and flaming rocks. At the same time, Mason was striking the groggy beast with massive force. Zaygoiphyth had only just enough energy to sputter out a flame when another stroke swatted him off balance. The vile savage was near the point of defeat when they heard a sickening shriek echo through the cavern. Zephyr regained himself and fought back. A cloud of dark magic wrapped around Aspen, stopping her from attacking him. It tightened and Aspen heard a loud crack come from her arm. She screamed in pain. Nixon rushed over, lifting a large rock with his powers. The rock hit behind Zephyr's knee causing it to buckle, he collapsed to the ground and the darkness disappeared from around Aspen but hit Nixon blasting him into the wall. He grimaced in pain but stood up.

"Aspen, I'll take Zephyr from here!", Annalise declared. Aspen nodded and ran towards Mason and Zaygoiphyth. She lifted her broken arm and her left arm. An orb of green started to form. She threw it at Zaygoiphyth, trying to tame him.

Annalise formed strong winds sending Zephyr staggering to the side. A cloud of darkness circled around Annalise's ankle, causing her to fall backwards. Nixon threw him against the wall with his telekinesis. Zephyr, slowly stood up and ran out of the cave. Nixon and Annalise ran after him. They stood at the edge of a cliff, glaring at the mischief maker. Nixon stepped back, knowing that Annalise could handle this.

Mason fought with Zaygoiphyth for a while, and Aspen aided him. She finally formed vines that twisted around Zaygoiphyths wings, legs, and neck. He struggled but Aspen stood her ground.

Zephyr and Annalise lifted their hands and a bolt of lighting and a cloud of darkness met directly between them. Annalise's bolt was overpowering Zephyr, and his darkness began to draw backwards. The electric discharge made him lose his balance and strength. Zephyr had sent one last thrust of his energy before he fell off the ledge of life and death. That thrust had been one final mark of his power, which was illusion. He could make you believe you saw all of your loved ones fall to the ground lifeless. He could fill your brain with images of the most cruel of injustices in the world. He could torment your very being with a sharp knife, and then you would be left in pain until something truly worth living for happens around you. His final launch of hatred for the world was hurled at Annalise. She let out a horrific scream, but in a few seconds, she crumpled to the floor, pale and internally agonized.

Aspen still had the vine around Zaygoiphyth to keep the him from moving and turned around to look at the petrified Annalise through the cave opening.

"Annalise! No, no!", Mason howled, gliding down transforming back into his stately human self. He seized his friend's arm and pulled it to his own chest, which was rocking back and forth.

"What happened to her!", he said, his grey eyes shining with worry.

"It was Zephyr! He blasted her right before he fell! You know what he can do!", Aspen yelled, keeping the vine in place. Zaygoiphyth struggled in the vines, desperatley wanting to be free. Aspen could see the pain in the dragon's eyes through the wet tears forming in her own. She let go of the vines which let Zaygoiphyth breathe. She walked slowly towards him, trying to push out the thoughts of Annalise. The large creature stared at her, its eyes red and scales grey. Aspen pressed her forehead to Zaygoiphyth's. Tears ran down her face onto Zaygoiphyth's muzzle, he closed his red eyes and she closed her green eyes.

"You're free" she whispered softly. Light rushed down his body, his scales turned into a sterling silver and his eyes turned to an icy blue as the spell was lifted off him. They opened their eyes and the dragon gave her a nod and flew off. Aspen watched, tears flowing down her face.

She turned her attention back to Annalise and ran towards her. The elf pushed Mason aside and pulled Annalise into a tight hug.

"Annalise please wake up...please" she choked, liquid dripping from her eyes. Nixon placed his hand on her shoulder, tears forming in his eyes as well. Wet droplets formed in Mason's grey optics. Aspen finally let go and fell into a hug with Nixon. Mason knelt back down next to Annalise and picked her up.

"We need to get back to Nightingael.", Mason announced. Aspen nodded, holding her arm. Their horses weren't far from the cave, but they had to navigate in semi-darkness to make it out period. Mason decided to lay Annalise across his saddle to keep her from falling off and lead her mare to Nightingael. He held onto the reins of her own stallion. Nixon and Aspen mounted their horses, ignoring their wounds.

They continued the hike in silence, pausing only to drink at a clear pond along the path. Annalise still hadn't awoken, but her breathing was slowly but surely getting deeper. Mason tried trickling some cool water down her throat, but it ended up choking her unconscious self more than helping her dry lips.

"Nixon, can you help her at all?", Aspen pleading while refilling her flask, gazing at her immobilized friend all the while. She remembered when Nixon healed her knee.

"I can try...but there is not much I can do for her. Zephyr's powers are strong, so no promises. I'm sorry...", Nixon said, hanging his head.

Aspen leaned over and gave Nixon a kiss on his cheek.

"It's fine" she informed.

As they neared the Central Province, they heard a voice coming from the somewhere ahead of them. It was a young man, and a young maiden. They were sitting on a quilt under a large tree.

"I'm so sorry Ayleth! I know it was wrong of to call you such evil words. I let my anger get the best of me.. I was wrong and I know that now. Can you ever forgive me?", the man asked helplessly.

The females hard expression softened as she said, "I forgive you!".

Just as the words were drawn from her mouth, Annalise opened her big, intelligent eyes with a start. True forgiveness was an act of real, plain, and honest beauty. That is how Annalise woke up.

The entourage hugged, and Annalise gave Mason a peck on the cheek for his heroic efforts. They explained the feat and circumstances of her fall while strolling into the city, prideful as could be. The team would never say goodbye, for Nightingael was forever their home, even though they knew the kingdom would never know why four dirty looking teenagers pranced into the village, one with a bandage around her arm, smiling ear to ear, their smiles being the only thing they could afford on that breezy Winter day.

CHAPTER 9

Struggle - Last Day of School

By: Keighley Byrd

My last day at Heritage Middle School was an unusually tearful one. Not necessarily from me, but all of my friends. I myself had a hard time keeping my composure. Carol Anne was the worst out of all of my fan group. She bawled the whole day until I had to go meet her homeroom teacher, so her teacher would know why she was crying, and more importantly, who she was crying about.

During first block, I was able to stay in Mrs. Reeves' room, even though that was not what my schedule said. My Gifted Language Arts teacher was nice enough to realize that I needed to spend time with my friends before I left for good. Most of my friends were in student council, which was held in Mrs. Reeves' room, so I was able to hang out. "Girls, be quieter. I realize that this is Keighley's last day here, but please, stop being so distracting!", said Mrs. Reeves. "Okay," giggled all of my friends and I. We piped down some, but we wouldn't stop talking. Finally, Mrs. Reeves shooed us out the door to deliver student council T - Shirts to the members who had ordered them. I walked with Carol Anne, half because she was my friend, the other half because I had to keep her from crying again. "That was the best first block!" I exclaimed.

Second block was chorus. Chorus was okay, but not as thrilling as first block. Mrs. Carter wasn't there, since her daughter, Katie Beth, had died at the beginning of the school year. We had a sub that day. She was nice, and she did help us work on our songs. She had grown to understand concepts like Solfege and harmony. She had practically been our teacher for the entire school year so far. Mrs. Carter had only been back to teach a few times. When I walked in, Avery announced that it was my last day at Heritage, so the whole chorus class, excluding the six boys, gave me a group hug! I was so overwhelmed that I hit the ground and the rest of the pack lay jumbled on top of me. During the singing of all of the songs, from start to finish, including "Happy Holidays" (we were practicing for our chorus concert), I almost cried. School for me and my supporters was very tearful indeed.

Third block was when the real class started. I had Mrs. Reeves (again) for Gifted Language Arts. This was more of a normal class period, though I still was given some privileges because it was my last day there.

Heritage Middle School seemed possessed by Chromebooks. Every student in Heritage Middle was given one. We all still had one, except for the few mischief-makers that had already dropped theirs. They had a problem. But for the most part, everybody had one, and they all worked fine. But on the occasion, they would act up, and we would need help with them. In this case, the students of Mrs. Reeves' third block class were not able to edit her file, that had been created purposely for us to edit.

Mrs. Reeves, Molly and I went to find a computer teacher to help us with our Chromebook problem. Me and Molly sprinted down the hallway, not caring who saw, until we saw a teacher of course. Then we cared. Once we found our individual, we displayed our given Chromebook, and set her to fixing our problem. Our dilemma had an easy resolution that was determined. Mrs. Reeves needed to turn on a certain sharing preference, and then share. Not visa-versa. Our complication solved, we headed back to headquarters.

Fourth block was fine and normal until the end of class. Brook (my soccer buddy/prodigy) ratted me out to Mrs. Montgomery. I had been a little scared to tell Mrs. Montgomery that I was moving. She was very nice, and I had a feeling that she liked me (all of the teachers did), but she was very vocal about her opinions on other students. She didn't know that I was leaving until that day. When she asked me about my move, tears immediately started flowing down my cheeks. "This move was not your idea, was it?" Mrs. Montgomery whispered. I shook my head in a silent reply. I realized that she was not a bad teacher at all. She <u>did </u>care for her students. She just had to act like a tough teacher to enable her students to do her work.

Fifth block came and went. Pretty normal stuff. Government, economy, and citizen participation. <u>BORING!!!</u> At least at the end of class, the whole class sung a song for me. I also got candy. I love candy, so I also loved fifth block.

Out in the car-rider line, Avery, my best friend (along with all of my other friends), had her brother, who was in band, play the Heritage Tribute with his friends for me. Avery's car came right behind mine. I was practically crying by the time I was in the car. We hugged for a minute then said goodbye. That was the last time I saw Avery that year.

Leaving Ringgold

The fact that leaving Ringgold was painful, came as no surprise. That morning, we skipped church to get the Ballantyne's house ready. Our house had sold in the summer, so we were living in our friends, the Berrys, grandparents house. The Berrys included Lexi and Micah, who were ten year old twins. They were the age as my brother, Myles. Then there was seven year old Isaac, who was my little sister, Camdyn's, age. Elliana Berry was the youngest at four, and was the same age as my little brother, Chandler. The Ballantynes only lived in Ringgold for part of the year. The other half, they lived in Connecticut. They did this so that they could see all of their children, not just one or the other. Around the time our house sold, Kathleen Berry obtained permission for us to live in her mom and dad's house. We lived there for a couple of months, and the house was more dirty than clean. But I do have three siblings, so I was not to solely blame. We worked for hours, moving things out of the house and sweeping, vacuuming, and/or dusting rooms. The work took an excruciatingly long time. But once we were finished I wished the cleaning would go on forever and ever.

As we drove away, I looked back at my home with tears in my eyes. I was longing to never leave, but I had no choice and with great hesitation and struggle it was my time to go. A struggle is defined as "to proceed with difficulty or with great effort." My struggle was real as I left behind and proceeded with great difficulty those that I know and love. My struggle is real as I learn with great effort my new home and look to make new friends that I will know and love. One day I know I will look back on my move and feel the bittersweet feeling that all struggles bring. I know I will grow, I know I will love and I know I will thrive in the end.

CHAPTER 10

The Jump

By: Tyler Callaway and Jacob Chandler

December 1984

My name is Devin Walker, I am 18 years old and have been on the run for 3 years with my 2 brothers Edward, who is 10, and Jack, is 15 .While deep in thought I hear sirens coming straight towards us, then I realized we have nowhere to run. Then a cop car comes and blocks the entrance and exit to the alley. A cop comes running out of the car yelling "FREEZE, POLICE," and I see my brothers sprinting right at the cop before I couldn't even had a chance to tell them to stop they drill the cop in the gut with a well-aimed tackle. The cop rolled out on his back got up in an amazing amount of time and whipped out his taser, and my brothers stopped in their tracks immediately.

A few minutes later we were on the way to the station but suddenly he pulls onto the freeway "Where are you going, I thought we were going back station," I questioned. "I need your help, my name is Mark Benskin and the fate of the world rides on your shoulder," he answered .My brothers went into full questing mode before I could respond.

"STOP, okay so where are we going then," I query, nervous about what he said.

"We are going to my house the cops won't find you there and you can repay by helping me save the world," he responded "and no more cops."

"Okay, so what is this infinite doom for the world" I responded sarcastically. Then in the distance I see a huge mansion that looks like it was brand new and it gleamed in the sun. The red paint was deep red just like blood. Not one dent was in the paint, the window sparkles as of a rainbow. I thought he was going straight but he turned right to the house.

"Welcome home," responded Mark as we pulled up right to the house. Then a garage made of what looked like solid gold opened up before he even pressed a button. It was like he had mind control. He said that it read his car and him with a scanner.

Once inside we saw a vast collection of gold and silver which never ends.I thought that hundreds maybe even a thousand people worked on this. Then he showed us to the bathroom where we showered and got dressed in nice clothes. Next he briefed us "So I have brought you here today for this reason, a man that goes by the name of the Soul Taker plans to make a laser so powerful it could destroy Earth completely, the only way to stop him is to find him first before he makes it. So I'll take the smartest to go with me to the hacking room where I will teach them the art of hacking. So which one of you is that person.

Edward barely able to speak mumbled "I'm the smartest."

"Okay so let's go and make sure of that real quick" replied Mark

"He hacked N.A.S.A of course he's the smartest and he already knows how to hack." I defended.

"So we have a rocket scientist do we?" answered Mark jokingly.

"Now Devin and Jack you both will go downstairs to the training room. Once there my assistant will teach you hand to hand combat and how to use several types of guns including pistols, rifles, and a mini-gun one of the most destructive," said Mark.

As we descended through the house I ask Jack if he trust Mark and he replied plain and simply no. As I took all that happened today we entered the training room with a vast collection of guns, knives , and more destructive weapons of war including a grenade launcher. On the wall there was a window which you can see a silo holding a bomb. As I saw all this I wondered what this guy did for a living.

"Hello, my name is Andrew and I shall be your instructor for hand to hand martial arts and weapons for your mission." greeted the instructor in a gravely way.

We soon started to learn the basics of takedowns, he first went to Jack but when he did a move he was thrown to the ground almost immediately.

"Where did you learn to do moves like that," asked Andrew.

Jack did not answer so I responded "he went online a few weeks ago and began learning." But I knew he spent 4 years learning to be a master in m.m.a. and karate.

"You don't just learn moves like that and I have never been beaten before so I will ask again where did you learn these moves" questioned Andrew.

"I have done m.m.a. and am pretty good at it, I also go online a lot so my brother is partially right," answered Andrew.

I saw that he was trying to not get me in trouble and did not want to get on this guy's bad side. So we went the rest of the morning learning kicks, punches, and other takedowns that were harder but not to the level Jack got.

"Time for lunch," Mark called at 12:30 and not a minute late.

As we ate Edward informed us on how he has already started to make his own systems that can hack the highest level of security, a top secret at least 10 times faster than other programs that are already out there. After lunch we begun weapons training, starting with pistols.

"Aim level with the head…." Andrew begun but he never had the chance to finish over the shots that ran out of my gun that never ended until I had to reload at which point I did it almost as fast as they show in the movies. And when we pulled the sheet back all you could see were shot after shot that went right through the head.

"So you only hit the head and can reload like Jason Bourne," said a clearly surprised Andrew.

"I took lessons back in Ohio in 2010, right before we went on a run that never seemed to end," I explained.

"I think you two are ready for your mission," exclaimed Andrew after day of intense training.

"Soul Taker has almost completed the weapon. You three must move quickly to destroy the weapon before it is complete and the plans. The weapon is being built in the Nekton tower in Zizalone, Ohio. I know this seems like a huge task but I know if you three work together you can save the world," briefed Mark as we walked to the garage. "Here's your ride" said Mark as we walked up to a McLaren P1, one of the fastest cars in the world. "the keys are in ignition and guns and grenades are in the trunk. Go do the world a great service." And then we left to go save the world but little did we know what was actually about to happen.

As we began to exit the driveway as we hear the bang of the bomb in the silo exploding suddenly as we then saw the mansion collapsed suddenly.

"Wow that was weird because we had just left. It's like someone has just tried to kill us and we happened to get out," questioned Edward.

But then I see off in the distance 10 men with guns and 3 helicopters flying above the mansion as if search for us when on the highway in front of us a tank was rolling right towards us then boom! A shell exploded right about 20 feet away.

"Step on it, "yelled. Jack and so I did hitting speeds of 200 miles per hour. Then another shell hit 10 feet away right behind us. Then Jack grabbed a RPG and fired as accurately as possible. Then the tank blew up and stopped moving almost immediately.

"They must have come to destroy us," said Edward.

"Yeah or the worst cops trying to catch us," joked Jack.

"Maybe we should at least try to get to Ohio," I Asked.

We soon arrived in Zizalone and found our target the Nekton tower.

"Let's just go right in there and destroy the weapon," explained Jack.

"Okay, Edward can you disable the security so we can walk right in," I said.

We then pulled out the guns and knives that were in the back and prepared to rush in. Then....... BOOM!!!! We ran out of the car and got out just before the car was just some scraps of metal left.

"Well too late to plan now, let's just go straight in guns blazing. Jack take the flank okay," I explained.

"Got it," replied Jack.

As we ran into the building we got our guns ready to shoot because we knew we needed to move quickly or this guy will destroy the world.

When we got to the door we let our guns have their first chance to kill. Then I heard voice over the intercom I heard a voice I swear I heard before but when the line went dead I still couldn't put my finger on who it was. Then we got on the elevator after not even a guard on the bottom floor. As we got on the elevator we went up to the roof and then about halfway up it stopped suddenly.

"Hahaha did you think I didn't know that you were coming. I have cameras in the elevator so I set up a decoy and setup men that will come for you in a minute so you have to fight and if you run I will just cut the line," came the same voice I heard just a minute ago came back on over the elevator.

"Where are you! One on one, mono y mono," Jack screamed.

Then the elevator began to rise and then we stopped on the roof where the doors opened up and Edward and I got grabbed and put on the ground while the man that we heard over the intercom revealed his face and we saw the man that we trusted and trained us,   Mark Benskin.

"Why," I asked cringing under the pain of learning who the Soul taker is.

"I did it because then I can show people cannot trust even the best of friends. I will go down as the strongest man in history, but first, Jack I accept your challenge," answered Mark in a cruel unforgiving way.

Then Jack charged forward and as if he knew exactly what he was going to do and sent Jack flying across the roof then I broke free and pulled out my gun and shot and hit him right in the shoulder. He pulled out the weapon we feared so much, the laser. It began to charge up then just before it fired Jack jumped in front of the beam before it fired and it hit him right in the chest and at that moment I run and hit him square in the chest and it sends him back and he trips and starts to fall of the roof when in that second I reach out but I barely miss his hand and he falls 30 stories when he hit the ground the laser gun exploded so the building began to fall.

"We have to get off," I yelled to Edward since the second he fell off the roof the men disappeared.

We grabbed Jack and jumped of the building undid our parachutes. When we landed Jack said his final words "I will always live on in your hearts." He died three seconds later.

"Now what," Edward asked. "We look like we just blew up the building."

"We are done running," I said just as the cops pulled up. I gave Edward a "just do it" look and we were taken into the policies custody.

But I wanted one thing "Please let us bury our brothers body because we know what we did and want to give him a proper send off," tears bellowing up inside.

Three weeks later.

"My name is Ronald Reagan and I know what you two did."

To be continued.........

CHAPTER 11

Anthrozoology: Go Look it Up!

By: Cadence Cooper

This is a story documenting the struggles of the many pets of my household and how they came to be part of the family.

Lucy

I broke out. That was the gist of it. I mean, standing in the yard *all* day was just...boring. I knew there was a whole world out there to explore (I could smell it). The world just had to be waiting for me to join it, and I couldn't let it down, now could I?

I was loping down a bumpy, dirt road when I saw her. She was a bit taller than my owner, and she was jogging at a steady pace, while still a faster gait than my ancient master could ever achieve. But there was one noticeable difference between this woman and my owner - I could feel happiness pouring off of her, in her heart, her soul, her whole being. I knew that this lady was different, that maybe-just maybe, I had a chance of a better life with her.

So I did what any sensible dog would do - tackled her.

A breath of surprise emitted from her lips, but I couldn't imagine why. I was simply making a greeting of happiness. I licked her hand as she regained her balance.

"Goodness, sweetie, I didn't even see you coming!" she exclaimed, though she wasn't mad. I could sense careful consideration in her, but she continued jogging, leaving me there, dumbfounded.

What had I done wrong? This can't have been what she had intended, so I followed her, sure she would come to her senses.

We ran for about 15 minutes, enough time that the woman was breathing heavily. I stuck right behind her, though she didn't notice me until now.

"Oh gosh - how long have you been here?" she inquired, "We're home now, you can't follow me-sorry..."

With that she opened a painfully squeaky gate, quickly closing it before I was able to follow. I watched her proceed to a log cabin with a giant yard full of delicious-looking sticks. As she reached the front door, she opened it, went inside, then shut it back with finality.

Somehow I knew she would not return for a bit, but I wasn't going anywhere. Not when a chance as good as this one had come up. I never planned to return to that awful-smelling, pristine place that I came from. Not now. Not *ever*.

That's why, when a medium height, bearded man came into view, I barked my high-pitched, one-year-old puppy bark. He looked over at me, but then went back inside abruptly.

Well, way to mess that up, I thought, once again depressed.

I was just lying back down in my spot when the door re-opened, the man appearing once-more. Only this time, I smelled something *amazing* with him: food!

I barked again, the man picking up his pace. I was *really* surprised when he headed toward me, opening the gate. He reclosed it, now on my side. I stared up at him, my mouth watering as I smelled the delicacies of the bowl in his hands.

We waited a moment, making eye contact. The man seemed to be contemplating something, and I sensed it involved me and the food.

He finally set the bowl down in front of me, smiling.

"Come and eat, girl, and we'll try to find your family in the morning."

You didn't have to tell *me* twice. I shoved my face in the bowl, lapping up the meat and sauce. Once I was finished, I waited, expecting more of this amazing substance that humans were able to somehow produce. I didn't know how it worked, but it certainly tasted good.

He seemed happy at my joyfulness, but then headed back inside. As he left, I noticed the gate was slightly cracked. Not too noticeable, but definitely there. Had he done it on purpose, or was it a mere accident? Sometimes I didn't understand humans, but I knew that this man cared for me, so is it possible that he wanted me to follow him to the house?

I decided I should take advantage of the scenario, no matter the intention, and I slipped through the crack in the gate. I bounded toward the stairs of the house, but the door had already reclosed. This was *just* great. I had a chance, but now I would have to wait *again* for someone to come out. I could tell it was getting dark, so I settled down in a cozy spot on the porch swing. *This is going to be a long night,* I thought, and with that, I tiptoed into a land of dreams (and food).

I was awakened by a light coming on above my head, though darkness still surrounded me. Raising my head curiously, I sensed the man that had fed me approaching the door. It cracked open, revealing his kind face.

"Hey, girl. How 'ya doin'?"

I looked at him, expecting food-or, more like *wanting* food, but I got something better: The man opened the door to the house for me to come in.

"Come on, girl, I can't stand just leaving you out here."

I obediently followed him inside, where there was a strong smell of a ginormous dog. *Maybe this isn't such a good idea, after all,* I thought, my senses confirming I might be right as the giant dog was revealed.

She was brown with a sort of black stripe down her body and tail, much contrary to my smaller, yellow self. Her long snout gave a menacing growl as I approached, astonished at her mere *size.*

"Now, now Dixie, it's okay." The man spoke to her soothingly, and then gestured at me. "She's not permanent. I just wanted to get her off the porch and inside."

Dixie seemed to be able to tolerate this, though she had made her point clear that she was top dog. She went to lie down on a hairy bed, and I settled on the cold, hard floor. I guessed it was better than outside, so I drifted off as the man went upstairs to his room.

I woke again to the astonished woman that I had seen running the day before. She spoke to the man, slightly mad.

"Chris, why is this dog in the house? She could have a disease or something!"

"Well, I couldn't leave her outside." The man explained back. "Just let her stay until we can find her owner."

The woman sighed. "Okay, fine. About that, she sure looks a lot like Mark's dog, Lucy, two houses down. Do you think we should call?"

"I already tried - it's not her. I can't imagine where else she would have come from. There are not many dogs around here as it is. Jenny, I mean, do you think...?"

"She *is* kind of sweet", the woman described, and I knew she was talking about me. "How would you like to stay with us for a while?"

I barked, sensing I had found my place. We all joined together for a group hug, including a little girl that had just run down the stairs.

"Hi doggy," she said.

"Welcome to the family... Lucy."

Socks and Blacky

The first thing Socks remembered was being nurtured by his mother. Soon Blacky came to her senses, too. They were in an old shed that smelled of manure and hay. They had two other siblings, one and orange tabby, one a calico, similar to Blacky, but lighter.

It seemed like an okay life. They drank their mother's milk, growing stronger with each day. Socks started to pounce on the rest of them, ensuring he was lead kitten. The calico seemed to get more of Mother's milk than the rest, so she was the biggest. Blacky was skittish and pretty much just hid from the rest of them. The tabby seemed only interested in cuddling with Mother. It was all going fine, until that one fateful day.

Mother left. Her purpose for going was unknown. All the three-day-old kittens knew was that she was gone. They waited and waited, but she held no return. Socks and Blacky grew hungry, and soon they were weak. They stumbled around the shed that they had grown to know as home, but no Mother was to be found.

The kittens could feel they were nearing their end when suddenly, everything changed.

It started with the bark of a dog. Socks, always the guard-cat, responded with the most ferocious meow he could muster.

"Did you hear something, Lucy?" they heard a man ask. The dog barked once more. Socks meowed, the other kittens joining in now.

"Guess not..."

Waiting in darkness for a minute, hope seemed to be lost when the kittens did not hear a reply to their desperate meowing. Blacky laid down in the corner behind a paint can, while the others whined in disappointment.

It was half an hour or so later when a noise shook the kitten's unstable shelter: Someone was trying to break in. Socks slumped to the door in hope, peaking through the shaft of sunlight that appeared through a crack.

The same man was back, peering through the crack.

"Are those... kittens?" The man questioned from behind the only crack to the kitten's freedom.

They meowed in response, Socks putting his feet against the wall to look through the crack.

The man walked around the shed, Lucy following him. He came to the door, and opened it with a creak.

Kneeling down, he slowly extended his hand to the orange tabby, who looked up in confusion, while still allowing herself to be touched.

"Hey, girl. It's okay - we're going to help you." The man pulled something out of his pocket and pressed a couple buttons, putting the object to his ear.

"Hey, so, are you and Cadie almost home? I need to… show you something."

After a few seconds, the man put the device back into his pocket and returned his attention to the kittens.

Socks padded over, sniffing the yellow lab that stood wagging at the man's side. The dog barked and wagged more, frightening the sensitive Blacky who retreated further into the shadows. The fat calico decided nothing too exciting was happening, and it was a perfect time for a nap.

A moment later, the excitement returned though, coming through the form of a woman and an excited child. The man walked towards them, smiling.

"Quite an exciting Father's Day - take a look." He stepped aside, motioning to the kittens shed. "In there."

The woman and child walked over, cautiously looking through the cracked door.

"Kitties!" The girl exclaimed excitedly, running toward a startled Socks.

"What… where did you find them?"

"Right here - Lucy smelled them. Their mother must have left them… do you think we could…?"

"How many are there?"

"I saw three - a tabby, calico, and a black one with white feet."

"We should at least take them in and feed them, then figure out what to do with them," the woman decided, smiling at her daughter toddling around the kittens.

They went away for a few seconds, returning with a light blue bucket. The man approached the kittens, pick them up gently, one by one, until all three were in the bucket. He, the woman, and the child headed up to the house.

A couple minutes later, Blacky stepped out from her hiding place, meowing confusedly at where her comrades had gone. She was getting hungrier by the minute, and she slowly laid down, hoping someone would come soon.

A teenage boy was walking down to the shed, and Blacky awoke with a start, desperately meowing for help. The boy stepped toward the shed, opening the door. Blacky slowly stepped out, revealing herself to the boy.

"Oh - there's another one. Come here, girl." He scooped Blacky up, and she was too tired to struggle. Soon she was on a bed with her brother and sisters, and they had all found their family.

Doc Holliday

I looked down the dusty, long paddock that I had come to spend most of my time in. I figured this life was fine. Sarah took good care of me, and I was in a much better position than a lot of other equines, but I wanted *more*. All those other horses got to run free, but I stayed, cooped up in a paddock, doing whatever *humans* told me to do. Though, through all of this, I knew somehow that my life would change, greatly.

And boy did it change. The first time I saw her, she came up to my master's door, knocking on it timidly. Sarah opened it, greeting the new arrival.

"Oh, Jenny, you're here - good. She's right over here."

The woman and Sarah walked past me to the barn, Sarah opening the door loudly. I knew another horse was in there, though I had never gotten the chance to interact with her much.

"Hi, Christmas Belle," the woman cooed, and I felt a surge of anger come from the horse inside the barn. *If I had that nice lady petting me,* I thought, *I would be grateful.*

I heard the woman question, "She doesn't seem too thrilled to see me, huh?"

"She's always like that with new visitors, not much of a people horse... but she really is great on the trails. I think you would like her."

"Ya... Hey, is that chestnut one you had out front up for sale, I might want to look at him..." the lady answered.

"He's... definitely... different."

"What do you mean, different?"

"There was an... incident... with another customer. She got on him and, well, he didn't like that. Took off on her, and she was a beginner. Feel free to look at him, but you can't expect much."

Somehow I knew the two ladies were talking about me, and my suspicion was confirmed when they exited the barn and headed toward the gate to my paddock.

"His name is Doc Holliday, or Doc for short, you know, like the famous cowboy."

The new lady gave a slight nod, extending her hand towards me. "Hey, sweet boy. You don't look so wild to me. She rubbed my face, chuckling at my lopsided blaze. I put my mouth up to her chin and gave her some of my signature horsey breath, which she breathed in deeply. I could tell this lady was special, though I didn't yet know if my future resided in her or not.

She went back inside with Sarah, and soon she was coming out the door, petting me a final time, and leaving.

Life on the farm resumed to normal for the next week or so, but I couldn't stop thinking about that nice lady. I had really felt a connection with her, so why was she leaving me? Maybe she would come back and visit again, or possibly even take me home with her - who knew? Until then, though, I would just have to wait and see...

My ears perk up as I hear a familiar voice. My lady was back! I neighed, catching her attention.

"Hey, Doc. Ya, you're the one, aren't you. You're so... friendly, and exciting."

She greeted Sarah at the door, telling her a variation of what she had just told me. They both smiled, heading toward me.

"Okay, it's your lucky day, Mr. Doc," Sarah told me. She attached my halter and lead rope and lead me toward an unfamiliar-smelling trailer. What she did next was perhaps the most exciting.

She handed the lead rope to the lady, who then proceeded to lead me *onto* the trailer. I couldn't believe it - I was actually going home with her! This was going to be an amazing turn in my life...

My lady took me to my new home, where I am still living a great life.

Snickers

I had a brief life before, but my life really began when I met my girl, C.J. She would do just about everything with me, trail ride, barrel race, anything we set our minds to, we could do it. I was sure we had a forever bond-unbreakable.

As C.J. got older, I noticed that we didn't ride as often, though she came out to brush me and talk to me daily.

One day, though, I sensed everything was about to change. First of all, C.J. was late to her morning brush. But I also noticed that when she came in, she was holding back tears. I wondered what was wrong as she came in and flung herself on me bareback, heading out into the woods behind our house.

We took our usual trail, C.J. stopping occasionally to hug my neck. I didn't know why she was upset, but I knew it couldn't last long with me around. I was right, though at the time I had interpreted that wrong.

A couple days later, C.J.'s sadness all the while growing, I was lead out of my stall and tied up on our post, encountering a different woman. She seemed fine, and I wondered why she was here, intruding on me and C.J.'s connection.

"She's so beautiful," the woman said to C.J.'s mom, petting my neck.

"Yep, this is Snickers. C.J. loves her, and it's really a shame to have to give her away, but I know you will take care of her. A little thirteen-hand pony is just too small for C.J. now."

"I'm sure Cadie will love her - it's always been her dream to have a pony. I have my horse, Doc, but it's time Cadie get one of her own. Where did you get Snickers?" The new lady continued to pet me, and she started to grow on me.

"We bought her from a family that had, supposedly, gotten her from Sonny Perdue, 81st governor of Georgia."

"Wow, quite a history. I love how calm she is… we might have a deal."

"Awesome… I'll go tell C.J. - this won't be easy for her, but it needs to happen." With a final smile C.J.'s mom went inside, leaving me and the woman outside together.

"Well, you might be coming to live with me and my daughter, Cadie, soon, Snickers. See ya' then, girl." I contemplated what had just happened. I didn't understand what the humans were saying, but I knew there was something special with that woman that had come to pet me.

The woman came back a few days later, and came to my stall to talk to me - C.J. and her mom with her.

"Okay, so Cadie's birthday is the 21st - I'll tell her the morning of it, and you'll drop Snick off?"

"Sounds good - C.J, you sure you're okay with this? We don't have to… your call." C.J.'s mom seemed assuring, though I still didn't understand why that was necessary.

"Ya, I mean, I hate it, but I want to do this for that little girl, because I was her once. Getting Snickers meant everything to me, and it will be awesome to provide that experience for someone else."

"I love you, honey. You made the right decision." She turned back to the woman. "Okay, we'll do the paperwork, and then she's yours."

"Oh, thank you *so* much. Cadie will be ecstatic. And thank *you*, C.J. This wouldn't be possible without you." C.J. gave a little sniffle, and threw her arms around me. I could feel that she never wanted to let go, and I didn't want her to, either. Whatever was about to change, I could only hope that C.J. would go through it with me.

"Alright, thank you for your business, Jenny. I'm sure Snickers will have a great new home."

I stayed at C.J.'s house for about a week or so, with hopes that life would continue as normal, and I would never again see that nice but evil lady that made C.J. sad.

Of course, hope is very different from reality. One day, C.J. loaded me into my trailer, but we went past the horse park. I soon arrived at a place that smelled strongly of cats, a dog, and a male horse. I did NOT like it. I proceeded to stomp on the trailer, wanting to go home with C.J.

As I was unloaded, I took in my surroundings. A little girl that was jumping up and down, and a set of parents, greeted me and C.J. excitedly.

No - this wasn't right. C.J. was giving me up, and I couldn't believe it. She talked to the parents, one of which was the lady that had come to see me back at home. The little girl came over and petted my forelock.

"Hi, Snickers. I love you. Thanks for being my pony." The girl wrapped her arms around me and, I'll admit, I didn't despise it. Maybe this new life wouldn't be so bad, after all.

The Chickens (Feisty, Six, Little Brown, Zebra, Sunflower, Stretch Armstrong)

It all started in a cage. The chicks heard lots of noise and bustling around them, and they felt a warm, red light above them. Occasionally, people would stop by and peer down on them, parents talking, children whining.

It was normal. Nothing exciting, nothing new, happened to the chicks until they were about a week old.

Two of the many people stopping by that day were a couple. The man had a big beard and shorter build, while the woman was tall and lean.

"Do you think these will do, Chris?" The woman spoke hesitantly, watching the chicks intently.

"They look good - just these six?"

The couple discussed it more, all the while the chicks going about their daily business. Soon another person joined them, sporting a red uniform that some of the humans sometimes wore.

"We can have them delivered to you this evening - we have to use a special transporter with the correct lighting since they are so young. Now, when you get to the location, make sure to set them up correctly. Remember - warm lighting, tall enough container so they won't jump out. I recommend a horse trough, perfect size."

"Thank you so much. This is for our daughter's Easter present - she'll be so excited."

"Glad we could help."

The people left, and the chickens carried on as usual. All Sunflower wanted to do was explore, while Feisty spent her time pecking on her sisters. Zebra was calm and delicate, contrary to Little Brown's sense of hyperness. Stretch Armstrong found his time consumed with a sort of meditation, stretching out his back legs behind him, and Six pretty much went a little coo-coo. She started running around, begging her sisters to play with her. They were definitely an odd bunch, but they were family.

A couple hours after the couple had left, two humans in the red uniforms came and opened the lid of the chick's cage. They all fled to the far corner, unwilling to be touched with big human hands the size of their own bodies.

After the hands chased around for a bit, a struggling Little Brown was lifted out of the sanctuary and into a smaller cage, still enclosed in a warm light. All of the chicks were eventually stored in the cage, Feisty having been the last one to be caught, unwillingly. They did not know where this new adventure would take them, but they were in it together.

Soon the cage was lifted into a dark room, and for about thirty minutes, the chicks were bounced slightly around, tumbling onto one another while a loud noise drowned out their peeping.

When the moving stopped, the smell in the air was different. It had a fresh, crisp aspect to it, rather than the stuffy, crowded place the chicks were raised in.

Two red-shirts came to the back of the room and opened a door, letting light in. The chick's cage was lifted and carried outside, revealing an all-new world.

In front of them stood a medium-sized log cabin with a big yard. The chicks spotted two horses who raised their heads at the sound of the peeping.

Then, the couple the chicks had seen earlier came out of the house, greeting the red-shirts.

"Hi, oh, I'm so excited. My daughter is at her grandparents' house, so we can set up in the back."

The chicks were walked around the house to an even bigger back yard, teeming with wildlife and happiness.

"Welcome to your new home, little chickadees," the woman welcomed. "It's going to be great."

The chicks were given to Cadie as an Easter present, and stayed in her room (in their horse trough) for approximately the first eight weeks of their stay at the Cooper residence. They were then moved to a coop in the backyard, providing the family with dozens of eggs weekly.

Edwin and Wendi

They started out in a big coop, full of other doves. They lived on a farm with tons of birds, and they were not nearly the oddest. From peacocks to guinea hens, the Ward farm had it all.

Edwin and Wendi were just a couple out of the tens and tens, probably hundreds of birds in residence here, but they were special. Unlike many of their companions, they would soon be going to live with a new family, though they didn't know it.

Mr. Berry Ward, accompanied by a little 10-year-old girl, walked by the dove enclosure.

"Thank you again for helping take care of the dogs while we were gone, Cadie - that helped us a lot." Mr. Berry absently touched the side of the dove enclosure.

"No problem - it was fun. I love animals, and this is a perfect way to meet new ones. You know, I *am* a Hufflepuff. Helping animals is what I do."

"Well, you're so sweet about it. Hey, I'd like to offer you something in return, besides your paycheck, of course. What would you say to your very own pair of doves? I can send some home with you if you'd like - I've got plenty."

"Wow, that would be amazing! I'll go home and ask my parents." The girl sprinted to the fence separating the two yards, hopped over, and headed toward her house.

Edwin flew over to Wendi, nudging her with his beak. She reached up and nuzzled him in the back of his neck, greeting him.

The girl ran back, practically bouncing up and down.

"They said yes, they said yes!" A man and woman trailed behind her, leaning over the fence rather than jumping it.

"Are you sure you're okay with her having them?" The man seemed hesitant, but Mr. Berry nodded. He walked into the cage, choosing carefully.

Edwin and Wendi sat in their corner. Edwin protectively cooed, bringing Mr. Berry's attention to him.

"Ah, you'll do." He carefully picked up Edwin and grasped Wendi, both of whom struggled unknowingly. Putting them in a smaller cage, he walked outside. The girl waited expectantly, smiling when she saw Mr. Berry approach.

"These are the ones," he proclaimed, holding the cage up for the girl to see.

"Oh, they're perfect! I'm so excited!" Mr. Berry handed the cage to the girl, who posed for the flashy light of her mom's phone. "You're gonna' love it here - I promise," she told the doves, who had just found their family.

Rocky

I think I had just about the worst start any dog could have. My first memories aren't that of a loving family, protective mother, or any of that fairytale stuff. I started out in a bucket.

I remember the loud sound of a car motor, a harsh voice, the desperate feeling of abandonment. Me and all ten of my siblings were sitting squished up in a bucket on a freeway, urinating on each other and whining our little puppy hearts out. I think after about an hour of that, I half went to sleep, half passed out. Was this really the point of my life? This couldn't be *it*...

I felt movement, like a gust of wind was pushing us, but we landed, still in our bucket, on the step of a big, stone building that smelled of chemicals and acid. I didn't like how it made my nose burn, but it was better than the loud motor sounds that had since been tormenting my ears.

We whined, hoping that maybe a better person would come for us. Hearing faint footsteps that got drowned out in the rain that started to pour, we whined as hard as 3-day-old puppies could. Finally, after a forever of whining, the door flung open. A nice-looking woman stood in front of us. Were we saved?

"What is... whoa, are those?" She knelt down, peering into our bucket. "*Puppies?*"

Another woman appeared, looking just as astonished. "What is it, Rebecca? Wait... did you find, are those... "

The first woman nodded. "Somebody must have left them here - we need to bring them in. She grabbed our bucket and headed inside.

I think I fell asleep again, because the next thing I remember, I was clean and washed, being dried by a little kid.

"What kind of awful person would do this to you, boy? I'm just glad you're safe now."

Me and my siblings slept in separate crates that night, and I had hope that things were better here.

I awoke to the nice lady from yesterday opening my crate, and reaching in for me. I gladly came, forcing myself into her reassuring hands. She carried me to a table, where they stuck something up my special area, but it was okay because I got a treat right afterwards.

After two days of a routine similar to this, something new happened.

I was enjoying my morning nap, when a different man came in the room. Not only was he different, but he was off schedule. I wasn't supposed to be bathed until another hour or so.

He spoke to a little piece of metal in his hand that I didn't understand, though I could hear it talking back to him.

"Ya, I'm here now. There are eleven total. Should I bring them over now? Are you ready? Okay, will do." He started to open our cages and put us in separate crates, 2-3 puppies each.

I found myself loaded with two of my sisters, both with blue eyes and light brown hair, with a little white belly. I myself was black with caramel eyebrows, belly, paws, and mouth.

We traveled in one of those awful machines that made the big noise, reminding me all-too-well of my first days on Earth. We sat in our crates for a while, finally coming to a stop at a place that smelled strongly of other animals.

The man unloaded us, carrying us into a building, where the pet smell got irresistibly strong. I didn't know what we were doing here, but I liked it.

Me and my siblings were arranged in a stack of crates. The people handling us seemed tense, like they were waiting for someone. And in they came.

A whole herd of people obscured my vision of the shop. Fingers were jabbed at me, and kids started tugging on their parents and whining, though one particular pair caught my eye. It consisted of a mom and a daughter, who pushed her fingers through my crate bars, but not in a jabbing way.

"Hi, little guy," the girl said in a lovely voice. I decided I like her. Wagging my tail, I pressed my paw up against her hand, and a connection seemed to flood through us. She smiled, and spoke to her mother.

"I think this might be the one. He has beautiful markings, and he seems to like me."

"You sure?"

I didn't wait for the answer. I knew this girl was my person, and no one questioned that ever again.

~All of the stories in this chapter are based off my real-life animals' struggles and fascinating stories, all of whom are still residents at the Cooper household. Thank you so much for reading!

CHAPTER 12

I Didn't Sign Up for This!

By: Jackson Foster and Evan McCarty

The date is 1939 September 4th: at almost the end of the great depression why is this HAPPENING?! HOW COULD THIS OF HAPPENED?! The world is in shock. Germany invaded Poland and started a worldwide war. Our president promises to not get involved, but everybody is scared. Still lacking money, we don't know what will happen next. Suddenly we are all bombarded with question that we don't have the answers for. What will happen next? Will they attack us and if they do and will that cause us to join. I would rather not think about it. It's scary just even writing this.

The date is December 8, 1941: I never would have thought it would come to this. The Japanese just bombed Pearl Harbor and the president is in an outrage. We were forced to join the war and soon they will start drafting us all. I'm scared. My hand is shaking. I best stop writing soon but I'm too scared. I don't want to be taken away my family. I don't want this for them or for me! I am going to stop, now I Must talk to my wife I can't take it.

The date is December 8, 1941: After losing many days of sleep I've concluded that I should spend as much time with my family as possible. You never know if you will be taken away to go to war. I am starting to accept the fact that I will go to war, but how will my children take it? How will my wife go on as a single mother of 2? AHHHHH! This is driving me crazy now I know why I stopped writing this, it enrages me and it doesn't do what I thought it would do. I thought it would allow me to get my feelings out in an unsocial fashion but, it just makes me mad.

The date is December 24, 1941: I got drafted to go fight in the war and I am currently packing. I can't believe my country is forcing me to leave my family on Christmas but I can understand it. My kids just went to bed and after I finish packing I need to wrap their gifts I'm going to miss them so much I can't even think about being without them. I don't even want to think about how I am going to tell them that I must leave to fight in the war. I just hope I will be able to see them again. What better Christmas present than not being able to see your father for years among years i am sure they will be happy.

December 25, 1941: I just told my kids that I have to leave today to go fight in the war, I have to leave in 2 hours and my kids are crying. Oh wait... the bus just pulled up, it was early! I didn't want to go without saying goodbye but I must leave. Please I just want to hug them one last time.

March 16, 1942: The training has been intense. I have been forced to shave my head and get rid of all my clothes and forced to only wear the provided military uniforms that barely fit. Me and my friends have been treated like animals, we barely get sleep, and we do drills and fighting simulations and it is just horrible. I can't stop thinking about my family but I have can't stop. The way they dragged me away from my family and threw me into the bus, I can't stop thinking about it.

September 23, 1942: I just received the news that I am being shipped out to fight in a month, and I barely know how to work a gun. During firing practice, I can never hit the target and I always lose in combat simulations. I just hope I will be able to survive and see my family again.

October 25, 1942: We all have just arrived at the campsite where we are waiting to be used as reinforcements. We can only hope that they don't need us. Anyways if they do, I better get ready. It is almost as if I am in school again. I have to carry around supplies everywhere.

October 27, 1942: I can't believe what I have witnessed. While we were in a battle, I was being shot at and my friend Dave took a bullet for me. He said that I need to survive to see my family again. I have never experienced so much death. Everyone around me were dropping like flies and I somehow made it out alive. Now me and what is left of my squad are being shipped out to who knows where. I just want this war to be over.

June 18, 1945: I've lost this book for years and I never thought I would find it. I have been training to be a fighter pilot for two years and I am going to be a copilot for one of the planes in the fleet that is going to drop the atomic bomb on Japan. It is codenamed "little boy" it is a very destructive bomb, a nuclear bomb. I am not sure If we will make it out in time.

August 5, 1945: Tomorrow I will be leaving to go dropped the bomb on Japan. I am extremely nervous we might crash or get shot down and if we manage to survive from that, we will probably die from the atomic bomb being dropped. I want to do it but I don't because I want to serve my country. But, I don't want to die.

August 10, 1945: When I saw, the bomb drop I thought why would we kill so many innocent people. But then again it will probably lead to Japan surrendering. There was such a loud boom that I couldn't hear anything for over an hour, not to mention the headache I had. It was horrible. Just to think all the sins I have now. How will god forgive me?

August 20, 1945: I am going to fight in one last battle before going home and seeing my family again. I hope I won't die in this battle. I was able to write a letter to my kids telling them I would be home in time for Christmas, they wrote back to me about how excited they were.

September 1, 1945: This is John's friend Joe writing. We were in the middle of battle and I guess he couldn't take all of the violence anymore so he got on his knees, stuck his arms out, and just let the enemies kill him. I think we just killed all of them and we are going to head back to base soon, wait what… there are people hiding in the trees I need to go before they…

John's journal please return to **** ********road (third house down)

Phone number   ***-***-****

CHAPTER 13

The Struggle of Finding a Topic

To Write Your Struggle On!

By: Sydney Harris

"The report is due tomorrow!" said Mrs. Roldings.

Paige Soft had just realized what her life had been put up to. She wondered why she never knew about this dumb report, it was probably because she never paid attention in class. She didn't even know what her topic was going to be. She brainstormed and brainstormed until she knew just what to do. She would take a trip to every single house in her neighborhood until she found the perfect topic.

The first house was the house around the corner. The one owned by the big bad wolf of the neighborhood. As Paige, approached the house she heard the loud barking of a dog. She feared dogs all her life but never knew why. She went up to knock the door but before the tip of her knuckle could touch the edge of the paint the door blew open. It was Aggravating Amy!

"I saw you walk up to the door and since no one ever comes here I got a nervous rush and rushed down here faster than Usain Bolt will ever run," said Aggravating Amy.

"I just came to ask you a question for our dumb report. What is a struggle you deal with on a daily basis?" said Paige.

"I deal with boogers, normally I just eat them, but when people stare me down I sneak up to them and put it carefully down their shirt," said Aggravating Amy.

"Thanks for the advice but I would like to acknowledge that I think you're an alien," said Paige.

The next house was my Memaw's (grandma). Whenever I go over there we speak Spanish. I knocked on the door and the door quietly opened. "Hola mi nino, tenemos tanto que ponernos al dia" said Mi Abuela.

"Yes indeed we do, but I have to hurry up so I can finish before night. What struggles do you deal with on a daily basis?" said Paige. "On a daily basis I deal with back fungu..."

But before she could finish I blacked out

"S" said mi Abuela. "Nice, but I have to go now so talk to you later," said Paige.

Now the next house is the house of my dream boy Cameron his eyes are as dreamy as the sun when it's dark or when you stare at perfect water. He is in my class and is completely single and he doesn't know I like him but I am seeking to tell him today. He has a younger sister her name is Raiein, and his parents are awesome.

As I approached his house he was staring at me through the window. I knocked on the door and it opened!

"Hello Cameron," I said.

"Hi Paige!" said Cameron.

"UMM!! I'm here to ask you two questions but I'll hold the second one for after," I said.

"Well, what is a daily struggle you have?" I said.

"My daily struggle is seeing you 24/7 you're so pretty. Wait did that come out of my mouth?" said Cameron.

"That's what I was going to talk about second because I like you! You're smart, athletic, and charming." I said.

RING RING RING…..

Three minutes later of talking on the phone with her mom…

"Cameron I have to go back home for dinner but we can text later if that's okay?" I said.

"Okay? Thanks for stopping by and you can text me later… Bye Paige" said Cameron.

"Bye" I said.

As I was eating my dinner with my family my Abuela interrupted and started talking about Cameron and how she saw me talking to him. I gave her a slight nudge to warn her there would be no coffee for her if she kept going. My parents didn't allow me to date which was so weird because they were allowed to date at my age but who cares.

"Senorita Paige you have a novio... You better not be included with that inappropriate nonsense. Do you understand me Paige Sapphire Soft?" said Mi Mama

"Yes Ma'am" I mumbled.

After dinner I decided I would sleep at my Abuela's house and talk to her about keeping her mouth completely shut!

Before I went to bed we had our conversation in Spanish.

{I'll tell you in ENGLISH so you understand}

"Abuela how dare you talk about Cameron and you said we would keep it a secret between US!" I announced.

"Miha you know I forgot. I'm so, so dearly sorry!" she whispered

"Abuela just promise you'll never say anything about Cameron unless we are talking together". I eyed

"Miha I will never say a thing again." she assured.

Later that night I found just the right topic to do my report on. The struggle of keeping your dream boy a secret from your parents. It was the perfect topic. As I woke up the next morning I printed my report and ran to the bus. As I walked into the classroom, Cameron stared me down. I got so dizzy but, before I could sit down my teacher said Paige Soft your up!

"I searched for a struggle even though I have many struggles in life I wanted to find one that happened that day. So, I went around to every house in my neighborhood asking for struggles. At the end of the day I found the perfect one. The struggle of keeping your dream boy a secret from your parents..." I announced.

Later on that day Cameron and I stayed up texting about how we like each other. Finally the moment I've been waiting for we were boyfriend and girlfriend but, how would I keep that a secret it was all a mystery?

P.S. Hiding stuff from your parents is not okay!!!!

CHAPTER 14

Worth Every Second

By: Mary Horton

"You know it's love when all you want is that person to be happy, even if you're not part of their happiness."

Julia Roberts

Power sequence starting up….13%…42%…. 63% ….95%…. Hello I'm Mitchell King. I am 16 years old and "upgraded". That's just a fancy way of saying part robot. Everyone says that it is a gift to be upgraded. I didn't believe that junk for a second. If gifted means getting stared at wherever you go than yeah I'm super gifted. Anyways, I was born with Parkinson's disease and and paralysis below the shoulders. Because of this,I had all my limbs replaced and my and a chip implanted in my brain to cure my Parkinson's disease. The chip has hindered my ability to feel emotions. That meant I couldn't understand complex emotions like love and hatred. My life was basically the same until I met her.

" Where there is love there is life."

Mahatma Gandhi

It all started with a bike. My Bicycle was broken and I needed a new part. Luckily My best friend Jonas's dad owned one of the only Bike shops in Arlington,Texas, which was where I lived, and I always got a discount at their shop. You would think that it would be impossible to find an old bike shop in 2050 because everyone has Hovbikes but there was the occasional collector that has one in their collection and needs it fixed up but other than that there was really not that much business. I was really their only frequent customer because one I am super clumsy,and two my bike is ancient. I got it from my dad on my tenth birthday. It belonged to my dad's dad and his dad before him. I never really rode it until my dad died. As soon as I walked into the bike shop I was enveloped in the smell of fresh tires and oil.

"Sup Mitchie boy?"asked Jonas

"Nothing much you?"

"I'm good,"Jonas replied"guess what there is a new girl."

Suddenly in barged a girl from the back room.She had rose gold hair and Sapphire blue eyes. She was wearing a white blouse with broad shoulders and the occasional grease stain and shimmery blue shorts.

"Were you talking about me?"she asked

"Yes we were" Jonas replied with a confident voice.

He turned to me" Mitchell this is Paris," then he turned to Paris and did the same.

"Now that you two have met let's go get something to eat,I'm starving" exclaimed Jonas

"Hold on I need a new chain for my bike"I responded

Then Paris yelled to the back room "One chain please"

Someone handed Paris the chain,I paid and then we went on our way to dinner

"You don't love someone for their looks, or their clothes, or for their fancy car, but because they sing a song only you can hear."

Oscar Wilde

For dinner we went to a place called the Daily News. No one knew what the name meant except for me and Jonas. Apparently there was this thing called a newspaper back in the day and people used to get them everyday. The only reason I knew was because I looked it up in my database. Jonas and I had come here so often that everyone knew us by name. The restaurant was part of an old broken down tram that was refinished by the owner and turned into a restaurant.

"Hi y'all how are you?" asked one of the waiters Kaze. His full name was Kaze Oxley But we all just call him Knock Out.

"Hey Knock Out," I said "We're good." He looked at Paris.

"Who is this fine young woman?"Kaze asked as Paris started blushing

Jonas replied"This is Paris. She is a new employee at the bike shop,"

"Well it's nice to meet you Ms.Paris.If you'll excuse me I have to go,but I will be back soon to get your drink order,"exclaimed Kaze

"Good," replied Jonas "Because I am thirsty with a capital K."

"What,"I asked, Paris and I were both giving him skeptical looks.

"It was a joke!Gosh!Tough crowd" Jonas said jokingly.

"Love recognizes no barriers.It jumps hurdles, leaps fences, penetrates walls to arrive at its destination full of hope."

Maya Angelou

After ordering our food and a quick explanation on who knock out was and ordering my usual, the meat and potatoes platter, we started talking about where Paris was from.

"I was born in Fresno,California And lived there until last month. It had always been my parents plan to move to Texas but I didn't think it would happen this summer,"explained Paris

"Cool"I replied "well Jonas and I have lived here our whole lives so there's nothing really interesting about us." Jonas elbowed me in the stomach. I knew what he wanted me to tell her but I just couldn't. The less she knew about me the better. Suddenly something popped up in the side of my vision. It was a message from my mom,it read"MITCHELL KING YOU NEED TO GET YOUR BUTT HOME RIGHT NOW." All I could think was maybe I should get home.

I turned to Jonas "Oh look at the time I really must go" I spoke quickly and then said my goodbyes.

"Bye Paris,Bye Jonas. Tell Knock Out that I will see him again next week."I walked out,got on my bike and sped home

" Love is our true destiny. We do not find the meaning of life by ourselves alone-we find it with one another."

Thomas Merton

When I got home I got the worst scolding in my life.

"MITCHELL XENDALIA KING WHAT IS WRONG WITH YOU?!"my mother yelled at the top of her lungs."IS IT SUDDENLY JUST OKAY TO WALK OUT OF THE HOUSE FOR FOUR HOURS AND NOT TELL YOUR MOM?!"

"I told Apollo to tell you I was leaving to get a new chain for my bike," I spoke with the most calm voice I could muster. Apollo was my dirtbag brother. He hated me I swear. He was two years older than me so I was just his lame younger brother

"Apollo get down here," my mom yelled up the stairs."Apollo why didn't you tell me your brother was leaving?"

"I don't know,"He responded.

"Okay well you are grounded until you do know,"she spit her words like venom into Apollo's face as if he was the unsuspecting prey."As for you mister,give me your foot."

I took off my foot and handed it to her. "But Mom," I whined. I knew it wasn't going to work but it was worth a try.

"No buts now go to bed!"

"There is always some madness in love,but there is also always some reason in madness."

Friedrich Nietzsche

As soon as I fell asleep I saw her. Paris. She was standing on a beach at sunset near the ocean. Suddenly I felt a pounding in my chest. We were the only two on the beach. Me and her. I was about 20 meters away from her. Out of nowhere I started running. I was running as fast as I could but she was only getting farther.

"Love is life. All, everything I understand, I understand only because I love."

Leo Tolstoy

Then I jerked awake. My mother board overheated and I needed to cool off. I checked my clock. It was ten past two. I threw my covers off my bed and went down stairs to get a glass of water and an ice pack. As I was walking downstairs in the pitch black I started thinking about my dream. What did it mean? Why Paris? Then Hit the ground with a thump. I forgot about my foot. My mom didn't want me to leave again, she didn't understand that I am a 16 year old and that she can't keep me trapped forever.I got up and got my water and the ice pack and then headed back upstairs

"Love is a fire,but whether it is going to warm your hearth or burn down your house,you can never tell ."

Joan Crawford

The next day things got better. My Mom gave me back my foot, and Jonas had a day off of work so we could hang out all day and I could talk to him about my dream. This time I told my mom and not my stupid brother where I was going. I mean don't get me wrong, I loved Apollo, but sometimes he can be difficult. Jonas and I met at a bakery two blocks from my neighborhood.

"Hey" Jonas Greeted me. He had on silver jeans and a button up navy shirt. "You said you wanted to talk so I came to listen.

"Ok" I spoke in a tense voice." I had this dream last night where Paris was on the beach at sunset and it was just me and her.Then I started running to her and then my motherboard overheated and I woke up."

"What!?" he asked"NO! It can't be! Mitchell are you in love with her?" He looked at me wide-eyed and just waited.After a few seconds he asked " Are you?"

129

" What no!" I said in my best cool guy voice. The truth was I didn't know what love was. I didn't understand it. I wasn't programed to feel emotion and so it meant nothing to me.

"So what is it then?" Asked Jonas "Why did you have that dream?"

"I don't know" I said frustrated." I can't explain why okay?!"

"Okay I believe you.alright let's go"

"Love doesn't make the world go 'round. Love is what makes the ride worthwhile."

Franklin P. Jones

That night I couldn't sleep. All I could think about was Paris. For some reason whenever I thought about her I got a message that said" EMOTIONAL STABILITY LEVELS DECREASED." Maybe Jonas was right. Maybe this is what love felt like. I doubted that I was right but there was a possibility. Perhaps I was just hallucinating after all of those times my motherboard had overheated. I wasn't sure but I knew that this needed to stop. I decided I would talk to her tomorrow.

"Doubt thou the stars are fire; Doubt that the sun doth move; Doubt truth to be a liar; But never doubt I love."

William Shakespeare

I was going to do it. I was going to tell Paris. I didn't know what to say but I was going to say something. I felt the warm, dry summer air on the back of my throat.

I wade a detour and went to a flower shop. I read in an article that the best way to steal a girl's heart was flowers and flattery. When I got to the bike shop Paris's shift was just ending.

"Hey guys" I greeted them as I rode up. Their shift was just ending.

"Hi Mitchell" replied Paris

"I was wondering if you guys would want to go get some coffee," I spoke with the most confident voice I could.As soon as I said that I sent a message to Jonah. The message said "Just say no." His tablet rung before he could respond to my question. He looked at me for a moment.

Paris interjected" I can't speak for Jonas but I would love to come."

Jonas chimed in " My dad needs me to help him close shop but maybe I'll catch up with y'all later"

"Okay we'll see you later" replied Paris in her usual soft sweet voice. I had never really realized it before. Paris hopped on her bike and we drove to the nearest coffee shop. When we got there we both ordered

"There is no remedy for love but to love more."

Henry David Thoreau

"What do you want? I'm paying" I told her.

"You don't have to do that," Paris replied.

"Yes I do," I said back to her. I was going to be that gentleman that I always saw in the movies who payed for food and drinks.

"Okay I think I'm going to do a Caramel Macchiato"Paris answered.

" I was just thinking that," I exclaimed. We sat at a table and started talking.

"So how are you?" Paris asked

"I'm good" I replied.

"Good" she commented." I really don't know know that much about you."

"Well" I said " My full Name is Mitchell Xendalia King."

" Xendalia, that's interesting" she replied " I like it"

"Thanks." None had ever liked my middle name before. Everyone made fun of it. " I am basically your normal, awkward 16 year old." I started to get nervous

" Same here" Paris replied " I'm just the weird new kid that only has two friends"

I looked at her for a minute. She was so beautiful and I was so...me.

"I don't think you're weird," I spiky with a soft sensitive voice. Without warning Paris reached across the table and grabbed my hand. I wanted to yank it away but this is what couples do so I would put up with it. Her gaze met mine and she smiled.As soon as that happened I got a ton of alerts in my vision like "ADRENALINE LEV-ELS INCREASED" and "EMOTIONAL STABILITY RAISING."

Soon she spoke "Mitchell I think I..."and everything went black.

"Gravitation cannot be held responsible for people falling in love. How on earth can you explain in terms of chemistry and physics so important a biological phenomenon as first love? Put your hand on a stove for a minute and it seems like an hour. Sit with that special girl for an hour and it seems like a minute. That's relativity."

Albert Einstein

When I woke up she was their waiting.I was in a hospital laying in a hospital bed that smelled like the stuff they used to sterilize it.

"MITCHELL!" She exclaimed when I woke up.

"Hey what did I miss?" I asked with a weak voice

"You've been unconscious for two days"she answered " so you missed a lot." Then she asked" why didn't you tell me you were cyborg?"

"I thought that you would think that I am weird," I replied.

"Well I don't" when she looked at me with her sapphire blue eyes I melted a bit but I knew it would never happen. Besides I didn't even know how to feel because of my stupid cyborg brain.

"I need to tell you something," she exclaimed.

"Me too" I agreed " You go first,"

"Ok"she said nervously " I think I am in love with you," I just stared at her in shock."now you go"

"I think I am in love with you too" my voice was horace and weak and sounded horrible compared to Paris's sugar sweet voice. I leaned in closer to her. I could feel her warm breath on my forehead. Then it happened. It was like whatever was holding back my emotions broke. I pulled her into a tight embrace. I could feel love coursing through my veins. I looked at her and spoke.

"You know you're beautiful right."

"You know you're cute right"she replied back to me. This had been the best moment of my life. Then she started to lean in closer. She was about two inches away from my face as Jonas walked in.

"Keep love in your heart. A life without it is like a sunless garden when the flowers are dead."

Oscar Wilde

"Hey Mitchell I…..WHAT IS GOING ON HERE!?" Jonas asked. " I LEAVE FOR 10 MINUTES AND NOW MY CO-WORKER IS ALL UP IN MY FRIENDS FACE!!"

"Calm down," replied Paris

"I can explain,"I said. I didn't want him getting mad at me. " Paris and I like each other, that's it"

134

"Wait a minute… YOU LIED TO ME THEN!" he quiet yelled. We were in a hospital so we had to keep it down for other patients.

"Jonas for some reason you keep forgetting that I am cyborg and I can't understand feelings like love"

"Sorry," Jonas replied " I forget sometimes" "Well I'll leave you two alone."

As soon as Jonas left Paris and I looked at each other.

"That was awkward," exclaimed Paris.

"Yeah" I replied

"Do you promise that you will never leave me." She asked

"Promise"

CHAPTER 15

Bear

By: Katie Lyons

I sniffed intently at the earth on the hunt for the wild and savage creature. My mission was simple, take out that awful creature, the squirrel. They may look all cute and innocent, but they are not to be trusted! I waited patiently. The squirrel stood motionless underneath the oak tree. Then, when the moment was right, I attacked. I howled in victory.

"Hah! You little good for nothing squirrel! I got you! This is was happens when you step on *my* turf!" I barked with pride.

When I uncovered my paws though, he wasn't there. I looked around. I snorted in disgust. That little rat!

"Bear! Beeeeaaaaarr!" Called Billy, the boy who took care of me. I trotted inside the small ranch house.

"I'll get that squirrel next time," I barked toBilly.

"Awww, why are you barking at me?" Billy laughed. I looked away. These humans never listened to me, but eventually I gave into Billy's sweet smile. I sat up on top of the sofa gazing outside. It began to drizzle. Billy sat down with me and rubbed my golden fur. He petted me for a while until he got up and went to his room. I thought about following him, but I stayed put.

"Bear! Want your food?" Billy's mom asked from the kitchen. I speedly got up and made my way towards the counter. As I chowed down I did some thinking. Billy's dad should be home, and if I see that squirrel when he opens the door, I'm making my move!

That night changed from drizzled to stormy. Billy's dad hadn't come home from work yet. An eerie silence fell over the house. I slowly approached the door, as the rain splattered against the window. I could see the squirrel. He was so close now I could almost taste it, That ugly little furball! He was about to get what was coming for him. Right as I was about to try and bust the door down using my ultra doggy strength, Billy's dad walked in, and as he did he left the door open.

"I'm going out!" I barked

"Hey Bear," Billy's dad greeted. I took that as a yes and dashed out going as fast as my long golden legs would take me. That squirrel saw me right as I got close and began to sprint away.

"You're not getting away so easily this time!" I howled leaping through the tire swing. The squirrel was heading right for the forest. I continued to go as fast as I could go. Leaping over roots and ducking under branches. The squirrel suddenly vanished within the undergrowth.

"NOOOOO!" I howled, "I have been beaten by that little furball for too long now!"

I stomped at the ground in rage. I didn't seem to notice until a few seconds later that James's house had disappeared. When I did realize this, however, I began to panic.

"Hello? Billy? Anyone?" I barked.

"Hello?" I barked quieter now.

Oh no, this could *not* be happening! I sniffed at the air. Maybe I could track them. I sniffed at the ground. It was dark now, and almost nothing was visible. The rain drenched my golden coat. I frantically followed a scent. Billy had never gone this far out into the woods. I had never missed home as much as I did now. Once I was too cold to keep going. I lied down, missing home more than ever. I missed my bed right next to Billy's. I missed the tire swing, and Billy's mom and dad, and the smell of pork at dinner time. *Yumm! Pork!* I thought to myself. I whined. *Where are you Billy?*

That morning was very bright, and the ground was still wet from the rainstorm, and so was I. I didn't think about that though. I thought about Billy. That squirrel! It's all that mangy little ball of fur! It's his fault. Squirrel's are the worse. I'd rather share a bed with a cat. As I walked around I thought. I thought about how I would have been a goner if Billy hadn't found me in the pound. I smelled. Come on super sense of smell! Come on! I heard a twig snap behind me. I froze and slowly turned myself around. There stood a bush creature! Well, it looked like a human, but with the body of a forest. The man had a contraption in his hand and he pointed it at me. The long barrel was pointed at me. I tilted my head.

"A dog? I thought you were a coon!" Said the bush man. He pulled the gun away and scooped me up.

"Wait a minute! Your Mr. James'a dog. He told me about you when he got you. Said you were a little golden retriever named bear!" The creature said.

He knew my name! He took me in his arms and walked through the forest. There stood the house. I jumped out of the man's arms and ran towards the house. Billy was sitting slumped over sadly on the tire swing. When he saw me his face turned into a grin from ear to ear.

"Bear!" He yelled. I jumped onto him and licked his face.

"You came back!"

"Always!" I barked happily.

The bush, man, creature was gone, but I will never forget him. If I learned anything from this experience is to appreciate what you have because it can be a real *struggle* without them, and also that squirrels are the worst.

CHAPTER 16

Right Brain

By: Amanda Robinson

Most people would say that Lillian Rossi was an average 7th grader. In her eyes she was not. She hated being left handed with her life filled with struggles. Lillian was walking through the lunchroom with her best friends Nina Centrella and Aaron Durham.

"Just look at it this way," Aaron tried to explain "You're in 12% of the population! That's more special than us, simple right handers."

"Well, Nina is ambidextrous." Lillian said "Which means she is in 1% of the population. She is WAY more special than me or you and possible the whole town!"

"Now I'm feeling bad about myself." Nina blushed.

"Sorry Nina," Aaron and Lillian said in unison.

The three friends sat down. A girl with blonde, wavy hair comes up to them. "So, how are the *3 Amigos*?" Lola Higgins taunted.

"Uh… Just fine thanks for asking," Aaron sarcastically exclaimed.

"I'll just leave you be." Lola giggled awkwardly and strutted away.

"What's her problem today?" Nina uttered.

Lillian, Aaron, and Nina were silent for a couple of minutes. They were sitting at a round table, all facing each other. Everyone at this school thought that this table was small, but yet none of the staff got rid of it. Their elbows practically touching, they started to eat. Aaron and Lillian bumped elbows.

Lillian stood up with an enraged face. "This is what I mean. I can't even eat my lunch without facing a problem! EERRR!" She stormed off to go sit by a water fountain.

Both Nina and Aaron walked slowly over to Lillian as if a bomb might explode on them. "I'm so sorry Lillian. We can talk about this later, it's time to get back to class," Nina said.

"Yes, it's time to go back to class. IT"S TIME TO GET BACK TO CLASS," Lillian exclaimed.

All three of them walked together to Mrs. Cunningham's classroom. Aaron said, "Looks like there's a new seating chart." Many people in the class groaned, but there were still some silent cheers.

The class was set up in rows so a student could either have a really awesome seat or be stuck with a horrible spot for nine weeks. Nina was on the left outside of row 2, Aaron was sitting on the outside right in row 4. Lillian was of course, in the very middle sitting next to all right handed classmates. "This is going to be a long semester," Lillian thought to herself.

Days went by until it became spring break. Lillian was laying on her bed reading her newest magazine when her mother walked in.

"We're going to Nana's house for dinner with the whole family so please remember your table manners," she said "We will be leaving in ten minutes so start getting ready!"

In ten quick minutes Lillian, her mother, her father, and her two twin brothers were in the minivan and ready to go. Lilian had on a floral dress with a pink ribbon around it. Her mother had on a black and red blouse with a pair of black pants. Her father was wearing khakis and an orange and blue plaid shirt. The 3 year old twins had on striped polos with khaki shorts.

When they arrived Nana walked out of the house and greeted them. "Your aunts and uncles are in the living room, but you can go play with the kids down stairs," she told Lillian. About an hour later it was time to eat. Everyone was seated with their food in front of them, they said a prayer and began to eat.

"Lillian," Aunt Erika said "Your cup goes on the right side dear."

Lillian knew this, it was just more comfortable to keep it on the left side. She listened to her aunt. This happened at all family dinners, she would struggle with this all the time with a family of right handers.

Before Lillian knew it, school came back again. The cycle of left handed struggles came back. Her reading class went to the computer lab to work on a writing. As always Nina, Aaron, and Lillian sat together. Lillian switched her mouse to the left side. Then Lola came up to her.

"Lillian, I don't know what's wrong with you, but normal people have their mouse on the right."

That word, bothered Lillian. 'Normal'. Was she saying Lillian wasn't normal? She thought about this all day, but Lillian couldn't get the thought out of her head.

Lillian thought that this was a normal day at school, but she realized it was not when she arrived at music class. "Today class," the music teacher said "We will be starting guitar, so go pick one up from the closet ." The students obeyed.

Lillian looked in the closet, no guitars for lefties. She gave out a huff. "I guess I'll have to play like this."

When Lillian walked into Mrs. Cunningham's classroom. Aaron and Nina were already there. " We've noticed how enraged you get when your left handedness gets in the way of things." Aaron stated.

"Eating at lunch, playing the guitar, computer mice, and nice dinners," Nina continued.

"So we talked with Mrs. Cunningham and she agreed to give you a seat where you wouldn't bump elbows with anyone." Aaron said.

"Aw! Thanks guys, I really appreciate it," Lillian said. "But it's time to go to lunch."

This day at lunch, Lillian and her friends sat at a rectangular table. Sme thing different, but nice. None of them felt like they were bumping into each other.

Lillian got home and a surprise was waiting for her. "Lillian come here," her mother said. Lillian came into the living room looking confused.

"What is it," Lillian asked.

"Well, you have always wanted to learn how to play the guitar."

"Yes," Lillian said with a questioning look on her face.

"So we decided we should get you a guitar for someone who is left handed." Her mother said.

"Really?" Lillian exclaimed. She saw it on the couch, picked it up and gave it a good strum. "Wow, thank you," She said to her mother. "I'm so excited to start learning!"

Lillian brought her guitar to music class one day. Her class worked on chords, she was so excited that she had a guitar just for her.

The day went on, she felt good about being a lefty. Until she saw that they had a substitute teacher. They weren't bad or anything, the subs would just ask Lillian questions that annoyed her.

When Lillian finished her test, she brought it up to the sub and walked back to her seat. "Miss," the sub said "You need to come write your name on this." Lillian came up with her pencil and wrote her name. "Are you left handed?"

"Yes" Lillian murmured.

As she sat down, thoughts circled her head. "I'm writing with my left hand, why does she need to ask a question about that?" She thought.

The rest of Lillian's day was normal, but when she got home it changed. "Hey, Lillian, how would you feel if I signed you up to have guitar lessons," her mother asked.

"Fine. Why?"

"Well, get in the car because you are going to a guitar lesson right now."

"Really?" Lillian said as she hopped in the car.

"Yes."

They drove off to her lesson. When Lillian and her mother pulled up Lillian was nervous. The house was a brick victorian townhouse with dark curtains in all of the windows. She walked up to the house and knocked on the door.

"Come in Lillian," a voice from inside said.

Lillian walked in to see what she had not expected, a light open house that was filled with light. She greeted the guitar teacher.

"You may call me Ms. Lawson," she said.

Lillian had a whole 30 minute lesson and then she went back home. "How was the guitar lesson," her father asked.

"It was amazing!" she replied, "I learned so much in only 30 minutes."

"That's great!"

Lillian told all of her friends about how she was taking guitar lessons. She was asked to demonstrate in front of the class, but the only problem was that she left her guitar at home. She picked up one of the guitars they kept at the school. Lillian held it like she would hold her own. She played the c chord, it sounded horrible because the school's guitars are for right handed people. In an instant the class started laughing at her.

At lunch Nina, Aaron, and Lillian sat together. "I completely embarrassed myself," Lillian said.

"No you did not," Nina replied.

"Besides, that guitar wasn't what you're used to ," Aaron said.

"I guess not," Lillian said.

When Lillian arrived home she told her mother about what happened at school. "You know, that being left handed isn't that bad," her mother said.

"Why would you say that ?" Lillian asked.

"Because National Left Handers day is your birthday," she replied.

They both laughed and smiled together.

CHAPTER 17

The Sister

By: Gabrielle Schlicker

Most people know about Bloody Mary. She was the demon from a slasher horror movie, the old queen of England who everybody feared, and the insane english woman who killed "heathens" for what they believed in. the thing most people don't know is that Mary had a sibling,a female sibling. Who was just as insane as she was,but for different things.

Mary's little sister was named Tabitha . She was born hating men. She detested men. If one touched her she screamed and kicked, foaming at the mouth. Eventually she was locked away to rot in her cage in the stone cold basement of the castle like a forgotten old pair of shoes. Laughing and screaming out her insanity, triggered by the guards outside in the hallway.

The fact that she was all alone in the basement didn't help at all. She was actually prone to more fits when she was alone. Tabitha would often rant about how invisible people were watching and laughing at her. Her only company was the four walls around her and the occasional rat that would either runaway ……or Tabitha would rip it apart and throw the bloody intestines at things.

Occasionally she would have visitors, like her father or sister. In front of

her sister, Tabitha was perfect-calm and polite with a smile and great manners. But in front of her father she was a screeching animal. Curses flowed out of her mouth like a river, with her teeth bared and eyes bloodshot and flashing.

As Tabitha grew older her fits became more and more violent, many times she tore up her clothing and furniture in her fury. Eventually the royal family was out of options. They had tried everything from Exorcisms to Leeching .

Nothing worked.

One day a young magician came to the palace, his name was Manja. He promised that he could "cure" Tabitha.

Mary gave him an ultimatum. "Either you cure Tabitha or your head will decorate the battlements with your blood as your body burns in the courtyard."

Surprisingly , Manja actually did cure her, and for exactly 13 years Tabitha was a regular woman. She got married and had two children of her own. And it was easy to forget that this shy, kind, young lady was a monster.

But Tabitha didn't forget, Tabitha remembered. And when those 13 years were up she went back to normal. Or as normal as she could be...

****

It was late one autumn night and Tabitha had just tucked her two little girls into bed. She was walking down the hall to her bedroom when she stopped, stiffened, and crumpled like a deflated balloon . Her husband, John took her to the Physician's clinic to make sure she was okay.

The clinic was small and quaint, with only two rooms on the first floor for the patients. Made out of wood with stone supports it was just big enough to live in with the second floor was converted to a living space for the Physician.

Tabitha was out cold all night and through the day. She did not stir and sometimes the only way to tell that she was living was her heartbeat and breathing. She was as still as a stone.

When she woke up, she sat up and hissed. John was holding her hand and he almost lost it. She had slashed at his hand with her nails and screeched, startling him. She scuttled out of her bed like a bug. Climbing up and across the wall with inhuman speed , growling and frothing all the way.

John sent for the physician and tried to calm down his wife but whenever   he got close enough to touch, she screamed and started to writhe and claw at him again. When the physician got there, he was stumped about what was causing it. The royal family arrived just as the physician was at his wits end.

Mary - now Queen Mary - knew exactly what was happening. She sent for Manja , but the foreign magician had disappeared as soon as he had left the castle.

Eventually the men left the room and Mary was able to calm Tabitha down. They used a root called Valerian to put her to sleep and tied her down to keep her from moving. Even in her slumber she still jerked when a male touched her or came near.

As Tabitha settled down, Mary offered no explanation to John or the physician and ordered them home. John protested and Mary threatened to lock him in the dungeon if he didn't leave Tabitha.

Once everybody had retired for the night Tabitha woke up.She was not happy. She started to jerk at the restrains, sensing the male guards outside the door.She wisely kept quiet as to not alert them of her being awake. Tabitha got free and raced out the window, leaped out, and finally screaming out her freedom to the brisk autumn night,sped out into the dark wood.

****

When Queen Mary got to the Physician's clinic in the morning, the Guards proudly announced that they had not heard anything the past night and the patient had not woken up yet. Yet when they opened the door they not only found no Tabitha, but also the restraints torn, window open and the room   trashed.

Mary scowled and glared at the Guards who were very suddenly rethinking their career choices.

They were sent to the dungeons to sit and wait for their punishments while new men were brought in.

Mary sent for her messengers who promptly appeared, having heard of the ones who had disobeyed or kept the Queen waiting.

She issued a royal decree, stating that anyone who could catch and bring back Tabitha alive would get their bodily weight in gold.

The messengers were sent out, each bearing a copy of the decree and a sketch of Tabitha.

****

That evening as people began searching for Tabitha, John decided to take matters into his own hands and conduct his own search. He had an idea of where to look for her at. A crystalline pool , deep in the woods where they had first met.

He was wrong, but not to far away from the pond was a cave and he did find Tabitha there. Her clothing was torn and mud splattered and her eyes were bloodshot and panicked.

As John approached, hidden in the deep shadows of the trees and underbrush, Tabitha cocked her head to the side, listening…..to nothing. She started rambling incoherently to herself, quietly at first but it eventually escalated into a shriek. She crouched down on the mud and hugged her knees to her chest, rocking back and forth, back and forth. Her eyes rolled in their sockets, almost completely red and their gaze unfocused.

John took a step forward, snapping a twig in the process. Tabitha froze, instantly quieting. She stood on wobbly legs, shaking like a leaf. John held his breath, hoping not to scare her off. Tabitha held still for what felt like years, scanning the forest around her. Seemingly soothed by the appearance of only darkness in the surrounding underbrush, she sat back down, but this time instead of curling into a ball, she lay spread eagle on the grass, acting as if she was making a snow angel. She started to sing " The Twelve Days Of Christmas" when John slowly let out the breath he had been holding.

Immediately Tabitha sat up, whipped her head around, and looked John straight in the eyes. She grinned, the bright white of her smile startling in the fading light.

Then she lunged at him, still smiling. She tore at his arms and face, leaving long gashes with her sharp nails.

The suddenness of the attack knocked John on his back with Tabitha on top clawing at him. He was able to get her off him and he tried to fight her off without hurting her, but it soon became evident that that wasn't possible.

He tried to force his wife from her attack but she didn't seem to feel pain and kept on attacking, even with wounds that would have incapacitated anyone else.

After a while, John began to slow down. He wasn't a trained warrior and in turn couldn't keep this up much longer. Tabitha was able to inflict more wounds on her husband but stopped abruptly.

She straightened and cocked her head at him. Her gaze cleared and became cool and calculated, nothing like the roving madness from before.

The last thing Tabitha said to her husband was in a honey-sweet tone.

" John it's not your fault, it's just that I hate men and you happen to be one of them and that just won't do. Sorry." She grinned at him and winked.

Then she lunged and ripped his throat out with her teeth.

CHAPTER 18

The Abnormal Atoll

By: Andrew Schnupp

The captain inhaled the salty mist of the ocean air, a breeze blew through his salt and pepper gray beard, while he looked through his lead telescope to get a better view of the oncoming land. "Land ho!" he howled. *Splash!* The anchor sailed down off the massive ship and plunged into the blue ocean water. Once the crew heaved the rowboats in the water, everyone got in and started to work, rowing the boats with the beat-up oars.

Once on land, the captain, Zant, told his head crewmember, Charlie to go and get the map. John, an assistant head crewmember, was Charlie's best friend. He was always ready for anything because he wanted to prove to Zant that he should be the head crewmember. Therefore, he had already gotten the map and handed it to Zant right after Charlie had left.

"Thank you John," he said

"You're welcome sir!" John exclaimed, the pride rung clear in his voice.

On this particular crew if you did not call the captain "sir", the rule was that you would be executed immediately with a sword to the head. Unfortunately, only one person had made that mistake; Samuel, one of the nineteen-crew members on deck did not say "sir" and he was killed on the spot. That was the first time someone on board was killed. The other crewmembers were still in shock over seeing the warm, oozing, red liquid seep out from Samuels's neck.

On the map, there was a jungle, a cave, and a big red X.

"Let us begin our journey," Zant told all of his eighteen trusty members.

The crew roared with excitement at the captain's announcement. In the jungle, it was extremely hot. All of the crewmembers were sweating and thirsty, they hadn't drank since they got off their boat. One sailor, Bob, had passed out due to a heat stroke. Of course, the pirates did not know that, they were as dumb as rocks. The exhausted crew had to stop their journey for a moment to revive Bob of his infirmity.

Finally, after walking for what seemed like forever, Charlie yelled in excitement. "I see water!"

Everyone turned their heads and dashed towards the lagoon. Several sailors were so thirsty, they stuck their faces in the murky water, not caring about the diseases most likely lurking in the dark water, and chugged. Once the pirates were done, and were relieved of the thirst that had haunted them, they set out deeper into the fathomless, dark, scary mysterious forest.

Naturally, Charlie had to ruin the dauntless part of the crew. "Legend has it that if you get lost in this forest, you'll never find your way back, ever."

"Nice going Charlie!" yelled the Captain. "You've frightened the crew! Now look, Bob soiled his pants because you intimidated him. You're an idiot!" The Captain muttered to himself something along the lines of, "Why did I pick this bunch of clotpoles?"

"No sir, I just had to go that's why," Bob said quietly

"Really, you couldn't just go behind this very suspicious looking tree?" Zant put in, gesturing wildly towards the tree. Zant narrowed his eyes looking closely at the said tree. "Well, now that I think about it, I think we should go check it out."

"My, my, my, this tree *is* weird," said John.

"Why yes, it is!" exclaimed Bob, his eyes too narrowing with suspicion.

At the tree, the crew eyed the small, hand-like hole in the middle of the twisted bark. Luckily, the captain still had his bravery with him and stuck his large hand into the hole, slowly but surely. Finally, after his whole hand was in it he screamed as loud as he could and his crew started to freak out and run left and right all over the place. One sailor even tripped into the pond, another fell over a log and tumbled down a hill. All of the while, the captain was laughing, doubled over his shoulders shaking.

"Calm down guys, I was just kidding, nothing really happened," Zant said hysterically, still laughing.

Eventually, everyone settled down, and Zant felt around inside of the tree his hand searching. Finally, he wrapped his hand around a large lever, and pulled hard; all of the sudden a loud noise erupted from the earth and then the ground beneath sunk inwards and a postern appeared, that led underground.

Inside the underground secret passage way, was dark and musty. The only thing blocking the sailors way out were the giant spider webs throughout the passage. They were the biggest spider webs that the men had ever seen in their entire lives! One man got stuck in one and it took the four strongest crew mates to pull him off.

"Wow, these are immense spider webs!" exclaimed John, the shock in his voice ringing.

"Yes, they are. Only a monstrous arachnid could create such an extraordinary piece of art." Charlie added in.

Once the crew had stopped awing at the giant spider webs, they continued their journey down the narrow passageway. At last, the trail finally started to incline upwards towards the outside, open world into the forest again. The instant everyone had made their way outside, they heard a loud monstrous roar and the group froze, not moving or making a sound.

"What was that?" Zant questioned.

"I don't know, but it sounds like it's a big creature sir," Charlie said.

"Well, whatever it was I guess it's gone now." Bob assumed.

At the moment, a giant spider came down out of the trees and crashed to the ground with a loud *thump*. The spider had razor sharp fangs stained with dark, red blood and they were bigger than two whole men were. The eight legs were coated with muzzled hair and dirt.

"Attack!" the captain roared, anger blazing in his eyes.

"Arrrrgggghhhhh!" the crew yelled in unison as they charged for the colossal arachnid.

Blades smashed against the legs. Blood sprayed. Arrows shot into the beast's eyes. With all of the roaring and the clinging of steel swords against the lower limbs, nobody noticed the five mangled sailors who had been impaled by the fangs, were now encrusted with their own dried blood with venom inside of their bodies. Unfortunately, there was no funeral after the remaining sailors finally killed the spider. The captain wanted to get to the treasure marked by the big X on the map so badly he did not care who lived or died.

"Let's go, I see the end of the forest straight ahead," Zant said not caring about his dead crewmembers.

Once they got out of the dark forest, Zant saw the same cave that was on the map about one-hundred meters away. At the entrance to the cave, there was an altar made of stone and a carved out man emerging out of the rock, in front were two objects on a pedestal: a dagger and torch. On the boulder that was blocking the entrance, there was a note that said:

"YOU SHALL NOT PASS.YOU CAN TRY, AND FAIL. ONLY THOSE WHO DESCEND IN KNOWLEDGE WILL MOVE ON!"

Of course, the note did not stop the thirteen remaining pirates from trying to push the voluminous stone out of the way. They tried and tried but they could not even push the rock a few centimeters away.

"Wow, this is extremely hard to move." John stated, eyeing the boulder and its surroundings."

"What about the dagger and the torch!" someone shouted from behind.

"Oh, I completely forgot about the torch and the dagger, maybe we have to do something with them?"

"I don't think so." Zant said.

"Why not, sir?"

"Because the note literally says, those who descend in knowledge will move on."

"Oh, sorry sir."

"There's got to be a key word here." Zant muttered with a puzzled look in his face

"I've got it!" Zant exclaimed after a minute of thinking in silence. "The key word is descending," Zant said. "But what does it mean?"

Almost instantly, Charlie blurted out "Oh! I get it! Descend is the key word correct sir?"

"Yea, that's what I just said."

"Ok, so do you guys see that man thing carved into the altar?"

"Yes we're looking at right now." Zant muttered impatiently.

"Well it looks like it's "descending" into the ground right there. So, maybe if we move the altar we could "descend" into the ground and a passage will lead to the inside of the cave from the underground."

"Hmmmm that seems very logical." Bob announced.

"I say that we at least try it." John expressed. "All in favor say I."

"I," Charlie said.

"I." John agreed.

"I." Bob joined in.

Moreover, a harmonized, chorus of "I's" sang out from the rest of the crew. "One! Two! Three! Heave!" Zant exclaimed as he and his fellow sailors pushed the altar to the side and revealed a secret entrance, leading straight into the cave just as Charlie had predicted.

"I told you, sir." Charlie smirked towards the captain.

"Hmph." the Captain disregarded that last sentence, and lead the crew into the underground passageway. Just as before, the passage was dark and musty, but there were no spider webs. In fact, nothing physically blocked the pirates from continuing their journey. It was just the giant claw marks that were all over the walls of the trail and, after they reached the inside of the cave, those walls. Bob felt the hairs on his chubby and thick, yet strong neck rise up in fear. To make matters worse, there was an ear-splitting growl and everyone's head turned to see a gigantic dragon that blocked the only way out.

"Nobody makes a sound," Zant said with fear in his eyes. "If you do we're all goners and we won't ever get to the treasure and be rich. Step carefully and slowly."

"Wow, these stalactites are really big." Bob whispered with amazement.

Unfortunately for the crew, he was so astonished with the stalactites that he reached up to the ceiling of the cave, grasped the end of one of them firmly, and snapped it in half. Because of this, two things happened; another giant stalactite fell off the ceiling, and hit a crewmember in the back. This sudden piercing pain in the man's back caused him to fall to the ground and die with blood gaping from his back. In addition, the echo of the piece picked off created a loud sound, which made the dragon open one eye to check its surroundings. When the random person fell to the ground, which also made a loud noise. Moreover, the dragon opened the other eye and leaped to life. Just as before, the Captain gave the order to attack.

"Attack!" yelled Zant.

Unlike the spider, the dragon was extremely hard to defeat. Within the attack, bloody guts were spilled everywhere because of the fire that the dragon produced. The smell in the air was a lingering stench of crisp, burnt flesh and bone. Swords tried to hit the legs. Arrows missed the eyes. No blood was sprayed. Finally, Zant ran and hid in a low level area inside the cave, invisible to the dragon, and his crew. It took a long time to notice that the Captain had gone missing. After some rare successful hits onto the dragon, one pirate finally realized that he had a satchel on him full of bombs.

"Light them up!" Bob screamed, swinging his sword at the fire-breathing dragon.

The man lit up all of the bombs and threw them to his fellow friends, who caught them and chucked them at every angle possible towards the dragon. *Boom! Bang!* The bombs exploded in every direction. The Captain, who was still hiding, did not know what was happening. He thought that the bombs were falling stalactites that had fallen from the dragon's fiery breath. Every bomb that was thrown at the dragon was directly aimed at his mouth. It took a long time, but eventually one bomb landed in the dragon's mouth and, just as planned, he swallowed the bomb. The dragon paused and started to choke. It choked, and choked, and choked, until the bomb finally exploded inside the beast's throat.

Splat! Splat! Splat! Bloody guts were splattered all over the men and the walls. Charlie went to walk towards the exit and tripped over the leftover head. It had one eye missing and the other was hanging out of the socket, dangling from a bloody string. The jaw had been blown off and there was just mushy muscle left. Charlie shuddered. Finally, the Captain came out of his hiding place and screamed in terror. Not because of the dragon, but because eight of his crewmembers were lying dead on the dark red smeared floor. They had been killed in action by the immense blast of the bomb. The only people left were Bob, Charlie, John, and of course, the selfish Captain.

"We have no choice but to move on," Zant said calmly.

"But sir…" John protested.

"No!" Zant shot back raging. "The treasure is literally outside the cave, let's go," he demanded.

Outside of the cave, there was a big, red, extremely bright, red X in the middle of the ground.

"We've found it!" John exclaimed with joy.

"We're rich!" Bob said cheerfully.

"Start digging, right away," Zant ordered.

The remaining crew started to dig, and dig, and dig, and dig, until there was a *Thump!* Charlie hit the object again with his shovel. *Thump! Thump! Thump!*

"Hit it one last tim….."

John did not get to finish his sentence when all of the sudden, *Bang!* All four people were thrown back and landed on the sand with a loud *Thud!* Each man had been impaled several times due to the extra pieces of metal that the bomb had caused to fly outward due to the explosion.

Zant knew that this was the end of his life. He felt sharp pain everywhere and long trickles of dark red, thick, warm, oozing blood. One piece, he could feel, had struck him in the heart. He did not know if Bob, Charlie, or John were still alive from the pieces that went in them, but he started to see a bright light in his blurred vision of a red ever-growing puddle surrounding him. Finally, he let the bright light take him away and recover him from his pains. That was the last thing he could remember. Then, everything went pitch black.

CHAPTER 19

Talk to Me

By: Abigail Schwindt

Peace treaty

We hereby declare peace between the two following groups:

The Twins

&

The five friends

Signed, The Peace Maker

This is a story about five girls who are struggling to get to know their new classmates; who just happen to be their neighbors as well. Though their struggle makes an unexpected turn, they stay together and work through it, but they never expected the new neighbors to ask for something no one would've ever have asked for after all that had happened between the twins and the five girls.

A long time ago, in September, when I was in the 7th. grade, a set of twins came to my class. I found out that

169

they were my new next door neighbors. I really wanted to meet them, but I had so much homework and so did they. It wasn't until April that my mother said that I could finally go and meet them. It didn't turn out as I would have liked. Here's what happened:

Lauren, Natalia, Makenzie, Camryn, and I all ran out to meet the twins, but they refused to talk to us. We invited them to our clubhouse (aka treehouse), but they never showed up. Of course, we thought this was strange, so we went over to their house. That's when they opened the door, threw a note out at us, shut the door, and said "go away." The note read as follows:

Dear Whoever you are,

I don't know what you want, but I can tell you that it is rather annoying to have someone knocking on the door every hour. I hope you understand that we don't like interruptions as we have a dance instructor come to our house to teach us dance on Mondays.

From,

The Twins

Camryn thought that this was very strange since we haven't knocked on the door every hour and we haven't knocked on the door on Mondays. This is because we have a meeting in our tree house on Mondays. Camryn and I went over to the twin's house and asked for their mother. She in fact did the same thing that the twins did. She opened the door, threw a note out at us, shut the door, and said, "go away." The note read as follows:

Dear Girls who keep bothering us,

We would love to be able to live in peace, but you have made otherwise. This upsets us greatly. You always interrupt us during dinner. If you would like to talk to the twins or I, these are the times that you may call us at (404) 345-2397 or knock on the door:

Sunday: Busy

Monday: Busy

Tuesday: 2:00-3:00

Wednesday: Busy

Thursday: 4:00-4:30

Friday: Busy

Saturday: Busy

Thanks!

The twins' mother

After that we never tried to talk to them again. But one day, we received a call from them saying that they needed our help. I was utterly confused why they, the twins themselves, would call me out of all the people they knew. What do you think I said to the twins after all they had done to my friends and I?

CHAPTER 20

Struggles

By: Nathan Smith

In a perfect world the sun would be shining, birds would be chirping, there would be no cloud in the sky, and I would be creative. Creativity does not come easily to me. If I need to be creative I can, but that's only if it's for grade.

Author's Note

It all started about… I don't even know how long ago. It's hard to keep track of time when the day keeps resetting. I know you're like wait, what? Before I explain what's happening let me introduce myself, I am NathanSmith. Ok so here's how it happened, my language arts teacher Ms. Summers gave the class a project that required you to be creative. That wasn't even the worst part. After she said that she said that the project counted for sixty percent of our grade. I knew I had to make a one hundred. So I went ahead and did the project. When the teacher handed it back to me it said I got a seventy percent. Then I was… sucked into a portal like object. When I got to the other end I was sleeping then I was awoken by my alarm clock. Then it struck me, that was the same day Ms. Summers gave the project. I figured it out In order for me to get out of this alternate reality I had to get a one hundred. So, I went back to school and redid the project with a completely different approach. The teacher handed it back to me and it had a eighty percent so I knew I was on the right path. When the day reset for the second time I wasn't surprised by my alarm clock. I went to school for a third time and that brings you to where I am right now when I got to my classroom I found my seat and and said friend Grayson, "I bet you were going to have a project that requires you to be creative and it will count for sixty percent of our grade." Then Ms.Summers said "Class today we will have a project that requires creativity and it counts for sixty percent of your grade." then my friend Grayson said, "How did you know that." I replied "How well can you keep a secret" Grayson quickly said, "I have kept one from my best friend since first grade" Then I responded, "Ok so, pretty much the day keeps resetting unless I get a one hundred on this project" Grayson looked puzzled then said, "Well that's unfortunate we have enough school as it is." I gave him a slight laugh.

Then I began working. I got it back then then before I even got to see my grade the day reset. I went back to school another time but this time i didn't say anything and just did the project in hopes that I would be more focused on the project, resulting in a better grade. Turns out that didn't help. "I can't do this." " I can't do this." "I can't do this." I exclaimed. This time I went to school with a bad attitude. I heard Jake the meanest person in the class whisper to one of his other jerk friends, "What's wrong with Nathan, did he not get a one hundred on a test?" he said mockingly. I glanced over at him as if I were saying "You probably don't want to mess with me right now". Then the teacher handed out the test. The whole time I was doing the project I kept thinking about what had happened with Jake and I. I began to take out my anger on the project. Not surprisingly that didn't help. So I need to figure out what I need to do first I need to have a positive attitude. Secondly don't get distracted. Finally add something new to this list every time the day reset. So I went to school with that list in my mind did the project and to my surprise I did better, but still not a one hundred. I woke up added something to my list and was off to school.

I did my project but, still no one hundred. After maybe fifteen more resets I had a list of around twenty things. To name a couple positive attitude, and read the prompt to see exactly what its asking for. I did the project once again and no one hundred. What was i missing? Then it hit me I needed self confidence. I am a very shy person and I often doubt myself. In order for me to get a one hundred I needed self confidence. So I went in did my project and there was no way I could not get a one hundred. When I got my paper I saw the most horrific thing i could a… ninety nine. I was so confident I forgot to check over spelling. So I went in did the same exact thing as last time but this time I checked over my spelling at least thirty times. I finally got my paper back and to my dismay I got a one hundred. Finally I got a one hundred.